THE LONDON

Bloomsbury, Fitzrovia & Soho

Lying between the worlds of the City to the east and Society to the west, these quarters of London have always been populated by ARTISTS and writers, VISIONARIES and intellectuals rather than by high fliers of fashion or of commerce. For all their glories, the squares of Fitzrovia and Bloomsbury, haunted by Virginia WOOLF, Lytton STRACHEY and the rest of the group, have never been the height of fashion and this perhaps enhances their charm as one of London's pleasantest areas for sauntering. Further south, in Soho, the pace quickens and the atmosphere gets SMOKIER and looser, like the inhabitants, from DYLAN Thomas in the Fifties to Jeffrey Bernard today.

The architecture is as rich as the literary associations, ranging from the classical COLOSSUS of the British Museum – with 6½ million visitors a year the most popular in the world – to the dreaming spires of St Pancras Station, epitome of Victorian GOTHIC. To the west, Fitzrovia has Pollock's Toy Museum, one of the smallest, in the shade of the BT Tower, central London's tallest structure.

These five walks will take you to the real Regency shops in Woburn Walk, unreal Tudor at Liberty's, the SIXTIES as they never were, in Carnaby Street, and the splendid Edwardian boutiques of Sicilian Avenue. MOZART, Shelley, a King of Corsica, Blake and Constable are met along the way, as well as the dapper SKELETON of Jeremy Bentham at University College.

THE LONDON GUIDES

Bloomsbury, Fitzrovia & Soho

ROGER HUDSON

Photographs by
JOE WHITLOCK BLUNDELL

HAGGERSTON PRESS

© Text: Roger Hudson, 1996
© Photographs: Joe Whitlock Blundell, 1996

First published in 1996
by The Haggerston Press,
38 Kensington Place, London w8 7PR
Unauthorised duplication contravenes
applicable laws

Printed in Great Britain

A CIP record is available from the British Library

1–869812–14–x

COVER PHOTOS

Front: The former Midland Grand Hotel at St Pancras Station

Inside front: British Museum, south front, with a sculpture, by Igor Mitoraj, in the foreground whose features are based on the idealised face of the Pharaoh Rameses II, met repeatedly within

Inside back: Bedford Square, a case of exaggerated entasis in Aberdeen granite

FRONTISPIECE

Fitzroy Square, with 'View' by Naomi Blake

CONTENTS

MAPS

Detailed maps appear on the following pages:

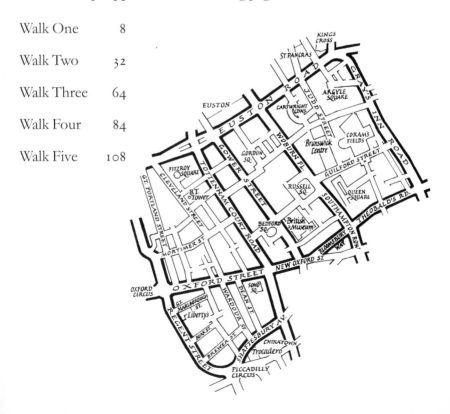

Start at the joint King's Cross and St Pancras tube station, from which you should emerge into the **Euston Road**. The Dukes of Grafton owned a suburban London estate to the west of here, and caused the New Road to be built through it in the 1750s, so that cattle being driven to Smithfield Market in the City could avoid the bottleneck round St Giles and Holborn. The New Road was thus the first bypass; it changed its name to the Euston Road in the nineteenth century, Euston Hall in Suffolk being the country seat of the Graftons When the railway age began they, and other noble London landlords like the Dukes of Bedford, were not prepared to be as accommodating towards trains as they had been towards cattle; hence the three termini of King's Cross, St Pancras and Euston lined up on the northern side of the Euston Road, some distance away from the centre of London.

King's Cross Station gets its name from a short-lived monument to George IV hereabouts, demolished in 1845. It was built for the Great Northern Railway in 1852 by Lewis Cubitt. His elder brother Thomas, in some ways the greatest of London's nineteenth-century builders, will be encountered on p. 41. Cubitt hit the nail on the head when he said his building would rely for its effect on 'its fitness for its purpose, and its characteristic expression of that purpose.' One of its two great arches was for arrivals, the other for departures, and the Italianate tower in the centre houses the large clock, so essential for an enterprise run to timetables.

The other element that now enhances the effect of King's Cross is the comparison that can be made with its neighbour, **ST PANCRAS STATION**, which at first sight would seem the product of a design philosophy far removed from Cubitt's. However, it has been pointed out that the position of the Great

The gasometers north of St Pancras Station

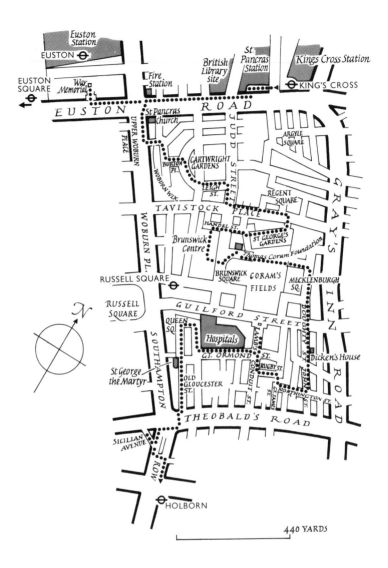

WALK ONE

Northern Hotel, separated from and to one side of King's Cross, is not so practical as that of the former Midland Grand Hotel, stretching across the ends of the Midland Railway's platforms at St Pancras, in the full splendour of Sir George Gilbert Scott's red-brick Gothic. And, however archaic and inappropriate such a style might seem, the huge, arching single-span roof concealed behind this frontage is an engineering triumph of the first magnitude.

As its name implies, the Midland Railway was not native to London, being centered rather on Derby. To begin with, its passengers bound for London travelled on the London and North-Western Railway's (LNWR) line into Euston, from Rugby southwards. As this route become increasingly congested, a new arrangement was made in 1857 to use King's Cross instead, but by the 1860s it was clear the Midland needed its own London terminus. The decision to go over rather than tunnel under the Regent's Canal immediately to the north dictated that the lines at St Pancras were at quite a height above the Euston Road. The lower floor created beneath them was not wasted: it became the perfect cellar for storing the innumerable barrels of beer from Burton-on-Trent which the Midland transported south to slake London's great thirst. Moreover, W. H. Barlow, the Midland's chief engineer, realized that the girders supporting the station floor above this sea of beer could form a ready-made tie to anchor a huge arched roof crossing the entire station in one leap. He was predisposed towards large arches by his association with the South-Eastern Railway's engineer, John Hawkshaw, who had recently installed large single-arch spans at Cannon Street and Charing Cross stations. Barlow and Hawkshaw had worked on the completion of I. K. Brunel's Clifton Suspension Bridge.

The preliminary stages of building were beset by two particular problems: the Fleet River, then a sewer in all but name, flows down the east side of the station, and great care had to be taken not to fracture the tunnel in which it was contained. Then, immediately to the north of the station its lines had to pass close by old St Pancras Church. The Bishop of London appointed the architect Arthur Blomfield, himself the son of a previous Bishop of London, to oversee the decent exhumation and reburial of coffins and remains from the churchyard; Blomfield in turn delegated the job to a young man in his office – the future novelist Thomas Hardy.

When Scott won the competition for the hotel, there were criticisms that he had gone way beyond the specifications to which the contestants were meant to adhere. (Much the same charge had been levelled at him over the Albert Memorial a little earlier.) One cannot feel very concerned about this because it gave him the chance to design a really major public building in a style of which he was a complete master: Victorian Gothic. Some wag at the time said 'C'est magnifique mais ce n'est pas la gare.' With no false modesty Scott himself said, 'My own belief is that it is possibly *too good* for its purpose, but having been disappointed, through Lord Palmerston, of my ardent hope of carrying out my style in the Government offices [in Whitehall] ... I was glad to be able to erect one building in that style in London.'

In 1872 the *Quarterly Review* carped that 'An elaboration that might be suitable for a chapterhouse or cathedral choir is used as an "advertising medium" for bagmen's bedrooms and the costly discomforts of a terminus hotel.' This ignores the fact that Scott's building is really quite unlike anything erected in the Middle Ages; he is merely using the Gothic vocabulary to sing a new and very different song. And what a wonderful song it is: London's most picturesque skyline, particularly when seen from the heights of the Pentonville Road; the mighty tower and spire at the east end, its clock faces always two minutes fast to keep passengers on their toes; the equally impressive tower over the arrival arch; the curving sweep of the south front ending in the porte-cochère decorated with byzantine peacocks and other birds pecking their wings round its capitals; the variety of the western side along Midland Road – a huge stepped gable, followed by an octagonal structure like some chapterhouse or the kitchen at Glastonbury until it reveals that it is sawn off at the back, then a huge chimney stack, before it tapers off into a series of arches, now troglodyte workshops for taxi service garages and panel beaters.

The Midland Railway may have refused to agree the estimates for sculpture to fill the niches, so that Britannia is alone in hers facing King's Cross, but there is a mass of other decorative carving to enjoy. On the west side look out for the stylized birds, six

King's Cross Station – the Italianate clock tower is a concession to the picturesque in this otherwise austere but pleasing façade

Less restrained, dragons, a lizard and a scorpion form part of the mass of decoration encrusting St Pancras Station

soaring up and six swooping down, above the first set of ground-floor windows. Here, as well as along the main frontage, at second storey level there are pedestals carved with rather classically draped females holding shields. And everywhere there are drag-ons, wyverns or other medieval monsters; particularly bony ones, some resting their clawed paws on their knees, support balconies on the main front, others are lurking under bay windows in bas relief. As you pass under the entry arch look at the passion flower with vine branches around it on the red cast-iron bracket, at the civic heraldry, the wyvern capitals, the brick vaulting. Then go into the booking office, done out in linenfold panelling, and resist any urge to confess your sins rather than state your destination when buying a ticket. The beamed wooden ceiling has gone but the stone corbels that once supported it are still there, some carved with Victorian employees of the Midland, equipped with tele-graph wires, brake levers, a guard's van, etc.

The ladies' smoking room (the first in London), the Moroccan coffee lounge and Venetian dining room of the former hotel above may be empty and echoing, but Barlow's great roof over the platforms can still be enjoyed, manufactured by the Butterley Iron Company in the Midland's Derbyshire heartland. Around the con-course runs a frieze, interspersed with capitals, all formed from variegated stylized vegetation. From here the Midland pioneered such innovations as third-class carriages on all trains, upholstered seats for all, and the serving of meals on trains, even if its reputa-tion for punctuality fell well below its rivals'.

St Pancras used to have as its western neighbour the Somers Town Goods Yard, into which came the coal, beer and other products of the Midlands. John Betjeman rhapsodised about the brickwork of the wall surrounding it, and indeed some of this still stands beyond the new **British Library**, which has risen in place of the yard. Whatever the promised splendours and efficiencies of its interiors, to be revealed in 1997 at the earliest although the original opening date was 1989 – the hall clad in travertine marble, computerised book requests, 12 million volumes gathered to-gether from 21 sites round London, 200 miles of shelving in its bowels – the Library's exterior makes a sorry showing alongside St Pancras. This was always going to be a hard act to follow, especially since the Library is in the same basic material, but the dire expanses of unbroken brick do send one's heart plummeting bootwards.

Prince Charles claimed he could see a resemblance to an academy for secret police. Now the hoardings are down, the effect is more of some haphazard sheds housing a heavy industrial process, cubes and lean-tos tacked on to each other in a random fashion, the only relief provided by the angled green shades above the few rows of windows. The grand metal gates on the southwest corner are formed from the words 'British Library' repeated eight times. The lettering gets bigger, thicker and more distorted each time until, at the bottom, it is a struggle not to misread it as 'Brutish Bray'.Certainly there is nothing to hint at the knowledge and enlightenment stored within, or indeed to encourage readers as they arrive each morning to add to that store. Nothing, that is, beyond Eduardo Paolozzi's statue of Newton in the courtyard, based on Blake's famous drawing – seated, nude, leaning forward, doubled over a geometric shape above which his hand holding the compasses hovers. In some ways this seems a strange choice because, for Blake (p. 111), Newton was on the side of darkness, 'embodying the evil power of the measuring mind', as Kenneth Clark put it. The cost of all this? £500 million – a hard sum to swallow, even with Newton's help.

Continue westwards along the Euston Road, past the shiny abstract sculpture called 'St Joan' outside what was the Shaw Theatre, shortly to become an hotel, and past the Arts and Crafts **fire station** designed by the architecture department of the new London County Council in 1902, to **Euston Station**. This opened in 1837 and so pleased was the London and Birmingham Railway (later the LNWR and then the LMS – the London, Midland and Scottish) at its achievement that it commissioned a monumental Greek Revival Doric arch, modelled on the Propylaeum at the Acropolis, from its architect Philip Hardwick. It is no longer there, and its demolition in 1961–62 in spite of considerable public protest did as much as anything to arouse the forces of architectural conservation. British Rail was desperate to rid itself of its heritage from the Steam Age at this time and another of its plans was to knock down both King's Cross and St Pancras, and replace

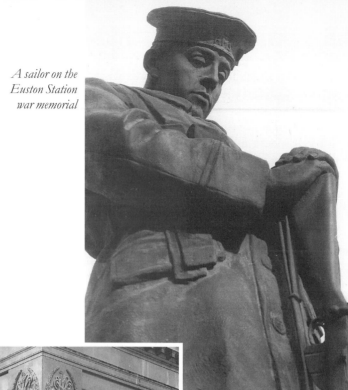

A sailor on the Euston Station war memorial

One of the pavilions flanking Euston Station, carved with LNWR cyphers and some of its destinations

them with a single station. The good news is that the arch may well be resurrected, with the help of National Heritage money, and thanks to the sleuthing of architectural historian Dan Cruikshank, who has discovered the whereabouts of much of the original stone. It would be positioned between the two pavilions, which are carved with the names of the towns reached by the Railway, and so framing the **war memorial** to its 3719 employees 'who served and died'. Good bronze figures of a soldier, a sailor, a member of the Royal Flying Corps, and of the Royal Artillery stand, one at each corner, heads bowed, rifles reversed, the ends of the barrels on their toe caps. The station itself beyond is a modern horror, a 'tawdry *ersatz*-airport' (Gavin Stamp).

Nip across the Euston Road, by the fire station, to another product of the Greek Revival, **St Pancras Church**. Partly because of the stop put to visits to Italy by the Napoleonic wars, Greece became a favourite destination for travellers in search of the antique in the 1800s. H. W. Inwood was among these and he displayed the fruits of his observations in this church, which he built with his father in 1822 to supply the spiritual needs of the smart new squares and developments springing up all around. A contemporary newspaper commented, 'It is a very elegant sort of place for a very elegant sort of party. It will do very well to read prayers in, and would be no bad place in summer to sip lemonade or punch à la romain. But it has little of the appearance, and nothing of the arrangement, which fitness and (we think) policy should have given to a parish church.'

While St Pancras, a 14-year-old decapitated under Diocletian in 304, might have been put at ease by such classical surroundings, it is certainly difficult to discern any Christian symbolism in the caryatids around the two vestries projecting from the east end, copied from the temple of the Erectheum on the Acropolis in Athens. These long-suffering girls were built up from terracotta sections around cast-iron columns, but when completed were found to be too tall, so had to be nipped and tucked round the waist. One of the original caryatids from the Acropolis is on show in Room Nine in the British Museum, and the St Pancras ones suffer by comparison. The church's portico, with its fluted Ionic columns, is also derived from the Erectheum, whilst the stages of

the tower are variations on another Athenian building, the Tower
of the Winds. Within, the use of large timbers in the roof allowed
Inwood to dispense with arcades, resulting in rather bleak rect-
angularity, relieved by the quality of the pulpit, veneered in
mahogany, and by the green scagliola (false marble) columns in
the apse.

Go a few yards past the church down Upper Woburn Place
before turning left into pedestrianised, flag-stoned, **Woburn
Walk**. This enclave of Regency shops, extending into Duke's
Road, was built by Thomas Cubitt in the early 1820s, one of his
first ventures in this area (p. 41). It is an excellent place for a sandwich, to be eaten while enjoying the cast-iron balconies and roset-
ted surrounds to the upper windows. W. B. Yeats the poet lived at
number 5 from 1895 until 1919, a long way from the bee-loud
glade, and the mackerel-crowded seas.

At the end of Duke's Road, turn right into Burton Street and
then left into Burton Place, which will bring you into Cartwright
Gardens. You are here on the old Skinners' Company estate, one
of the City livery companies, and it was developed for them by
James Burton. He was a Scot, born Haliburton, who came to
prominence in the 1790s, building nearly 600 houses on the
Foundling Hospital's land to the south-east. Until 1817 he was
also the dominant builder on the Duke of Bedford's Bloomsbury
Estate, speeding the erection of his terraces by involving numbers
of smaller builders and by the mass production of iron and woodwork off-site. His son Decimus is better remembered these days,
but the father should not be forgotten in this neighbourhood.

Cartwright Gardens is a decent-enough early nineteenth-
century (1807) crescent, but cluttered with the signs of the small
hotels which always appear like a rash near any London railway
station. (A little to the east, Argyle Square (1820s) suffers from the
same complaint.) The statue sharing the crescent garden with two
tennis courts is of John Cartwright. He retired from the Royal
Navy in 1776 because he could not stomach fighting against the
American colonists. He then earned his title as the Father of
Reform by being 'the firm, consistent and persevering advocate of
universal suffrage, equal representation, vote by ballot and annual
parliaments'. He lived in Burton Crescent (as Cartwright Gardens

Caryatids at St Pancras Church

Regency shops in Duke's Road, the continuation of Woburn Walk

was then called) from 1819 until his death in 1824. His brother
Edmund, a parson, is just as interesting a figure by virtue of being
the inventor of two of the key devices of the Industrial Revolution: the power loom and the wool combing machine. In 1800 the
5th Duke of Bedford, whose statue will be encountered at the
southern end of Russell Square (p. 47), made him manager of the
experimental farm on his country estate at Woburn in Bedford-
shire.

Down **Leigh Street**, past the olive-and-blue-tiled Norfolk
Arms, to **Judd Street** where it is worth diverting northwards to
look at number 95 and its Corinthian-columned early nineteenth-
century shopfront. Then back southwards before turning left into
Tavistock Place, which soon becomes **Regent Square**. Only the
south side is original; St Peter's, another church by H. W. Inwood
on the east side, was bombed and then its Ionic-columned portico, which had survived, was destroyed in 1967. Bereft of this
redeeming feature and with its garden surrounded by a wire chain-
link fence, Regent Square has little to offer now apart from the
message that

> Bates's salve cures
> Wounds and sores

painted in faded lettering on a building end. At the south-eastern
corner of Regent Square there is an easily missed gateway leading
into **St George's Gardens**. This was established as a burial
ground for the two new eighteenth-century churches of St
George, Bloomsbury and St George the Martyr, Queen Square. It
is a long time since any burials took place and its gravestones, their
inscriptions largely illegible, have been moved to the edge, leaving
only the odd ivy-clad table tomb among the plane trees, a
grandiose obelisk and, incongruously, a late-Victorian terracotta
statue of Euterpe, one of the nine Muses, rescued from the Apollo
pub in the Tottenham Court Road when it was demolished in
1961. The Revd Sydney Smith, sometime denizen of Doughty
Street (p. 25), once remarked on how much more pleasant the
world would be, were there only 9 Articles and 39 Muses, instead
of the reverse, so would have approved of her presence. The best
of the table tombs, with a pyramidical top and a curiously eroded

*The Muse Euterpe gazes serenely
over St George's Gardens*

*In Kenton Street, north
of the Brunswick Centre*

The Brunswick Centre

A mews entry, belying its name, off Grenville Street, Brunswick Square

coat of arms, houses the remains of Anna, sixth daughter of Richard Cromwell. Tumbledown Dick, as he was called, inherited the title of Lord Protector on his father Oliver's death in 1658, but he 'had not a spirit fit to succeed his father, or to manage such a perplexed government' and soon was out of office, 'a wretch who durst not reign' (Mrs Lucy Hutchinson). It seems probable that the bodies of two Jacobite officers, executed in London after the 1745 rebellion, were buried here, while their heads were the last to be exposed on Temple Bar at the west end of Fleet Street.

Leave the Gardens at their western end and walk down Handel Street until the **Brunswick Centre** appears on your left. This massive arrangement of tiers of flats, stepped back from a central pedestrian avenue of shops, was a brave attempt in the early 1970s at a new type of urban housing. In certain lights it still has some of the potency of a Mayan ball court rising out of the Mexican scrub, but it suffers from the smears, dribbles and under-arm stains which seem inseparable from concrete constructions, and the general level of maintenance in the public areas is deplorable. Camden Council seem to have given up on the raised flower beds, shrubs and tubs.

Go out by the entrance to the Renoir underground cinema and along the north side of **Brunswick Square**. George IV married his first cousin, second wife, and subsequent loose cannon, Caroline of Brunswick, in 1795, which tells us when this and its twin, Mecklenburgh Square (named after his mother, Charlotte of Mecklenburg-Strelitz) were conceived by Samuel Pepys Cockerell (p. 103), architect to the **FOUNDLING HOSPITAL** estate. The Hospital buildings, already extant, were to be set off by a square to either side, the whole making an impressive entity when viewed from, say, Guilford Street to the south. In 1911–12, number 38 on the northern side of Brunswick Square, which no longer exists, was home to Virginia Woolf, her brother Adrian Stephen, J. M. Keynes the economist, Duncan Grant the painter, and the man who was shortly to become her husband, Leonard Woolf.

In Jane Austen's novel *Emma*, Emma's sister Isabella Knightley lives in Brunswick Square: 'You must not confound us with London in general, my dear sir. The neighbourhood of Brunswick Square is very different from almost all the rest . . . we are so remarkably airy!' True enough, when the fields started behind the Hospital and stretched up to hilly Hampstead, but by 1926 they had long been swallowed up and the atmosphere was full of smoke. It was this that persuaded the governors of the Foundling Hospital to move the children in their care out of London to new premises in Berkhamsted. The eighteenth-century Hospital buildings were demolished, alas, and only thanks to the efforts of Lord Rothermere and others were Coram Fields, the children's playground between the two squares, preserved.

Captain Thomas Coram came back to London in 1719, having made his fortune shipbuilding in New England. He become distressed by the sight of babies exposed to die by the roadside, enlisted the support of the fashionable and aristocratic world and eventually the 'hospital' for these 'foundlings' opened its doors in Hatton Garden in 1741, before moving here in 1745. Once received, the babies were then placed with wet nurses in the country round about for their first five years before returning to be brought up in the Hospital. Mortality levels were horrifically high by our standards, with only a third of the children surviving to the point where they could be apprenticed to learn a trade, join a regimental band, or go into domestic service.

Number 40, on the north side of Brunswick Square, was built in 1937 as its London headquarters by the charity, which altered its name to the Thomas Coram Foundation in 1953. William Hogarth was associated with the Hospital from the start, and realised that it could be a showcase for his fellow artists (who had no other venue for public exhibitions), since so many rich potential patrons came to visit this new, fashionable attraction. The fruits of this clever piece of marketing are still to be seen at number 40 (phone 0171 278 2424 to check when open) in the Court Room, Committee Room and Picture Gallery there. The Court Room, with its magnificent rococo plasterwork, was preserved when the Hospital was demolished, and then re-erected, as was the fine oak staircase. It has an overmantel carved by Rysbrack, whose monuments feature so prominently in Westminster Abbey. There are large oils on Biblical themes, but more interesting are the small oval views of other London hospitals, including two by Richard Wilson (p. 68) and one by Gainsborough.

Brunswick Square

*Mecklenburgh Square,
east side*

The two outstanding Hogarths are his portrait of Thomas Coram and his *March of the Guards to Finchley*. This shows the scene in the Tottenham Court Road in September 1745 as the soldiers made their way to the mustering point, whence they would go further north to confront Bonnie Prince Charlie's Highlanders. In fact the Jacobite army came no further south than Derby, before turning for home. Handel gave many performances of the *Messiah* for the benefit of the Hospital, and there is a fine terracotta bust of him by Roubiliac, as a reminder of that connection. Perhaps the best of the other paintings at the Foundation are Allan Ramsay's portrait of Dr Mead (1747), a leading physician of the day, and Charles Brooking's sea piece (1754).

The most moving exhibits are the trinkets, coins, ribbons, etc, left two hundred years ago as identifying tokens by mothers, in the hope that they might come back and reclaim their offspring in better days. The mother of child number 734 left a verse:

> Who breathes must suffer.
> Who thinks must mourn.
> And he alone is blest
> Who ne'er was born.

The Foundation no longer runs an orphanage, but continues its work with needy and deprived children.

Turn left out of the Foundation, and cut through to **Mecklenburgh Square** by the path alongside the all-weather sports pitches. In 1939, Virginia and Leonard Woolf moved themselves and their publishing firm, the Hogarth Press, to number 37 on the north side of the Square (since rebuilt), driven out of Tavistock Square by threats of development and increasing traffic noise. Once there, Virginia Woolf was soon noting the effects of the war: 'very stout women wear blue trousers. No one ever sits down.' The east side of the Square was built by Joseph Kay, S. P. Cockerell's pupil, in the 1800s, and he borrowed much of the detail of this stucco terrace from Robert Adam's east side of Fitzroy Square (p. 79), built about fifteen years earlier. The large block on the south side of the square is London House, for London University's overseas graduate students, by Sir Herbert Baker, redeemed by its grassy quadrangle and knapped flint ground floor.

Down **Doughty Street** to number 14, on the left, where the Smith of Smiths (as Macaulay called him), the Revd **Sydney Smith**, lived between 1803 and 1806. The wittiest of men, he must have been happy here since he characterised the country as 'a kind of healthy grave' and said that, when in it, 'I always fear that creation will expire before teatime.' To begin with, though, he was very improverished, until appointed to preach at certain times in chapels in Mayfair and Fitzroy Square, and then at the Foundling Hospital. His prospects of further clerical preferment were hindered by a sermon he preached in favour of Roman Catholic emancipation: 'I think I shall remain long as I am. I have no powerful friends. I belong to no party. I do not cant.' However, a series of lectures on moral philosophy which he gave at the Royal Institution in Albemarle Street in 1804 made him the talk of the town, and in 1806 he was able to move west to Portman Square.

Practically opposite is number 48, the **Dickens House Museum**, where the novelist went to live at the start of the second year of his marriage in 1837. Here he completed *Pickwick Papers*, wrote all of *Oliver Twist*, most of *Nicholas Nickleby* and began *Barnaby Rudge*, before a growing family and increasing wealth took him to Regent's Park in 1839. Little attempt has been made to recreate the appearance of the interior as it would have been then, except for the first-floor front drawing room. And even there, the effect is rather spoilt by the ugly glass and metal barrier behind which the visitor stands. The other rooms are given over to displays of Dickensiana of every type, with lino underfoot. But of course, if you have fallen under the man's spell, it is well worth a visit. The originals of some of Phiz's illustrations for the books are particularly interesting.

Continue southwards along Doughty Street, which is still home to the *Spectator* magazine and once also claimed the *Pigeon Fancier's Gazette*, published by the Coo Press. Where Doughty Street changes its name to John Street, notice the two good 1930s stone female nudes at the top of the columns either side of the door to number 21. Then go right along Northington Street until it reaches **Great James Street**. This is one of a number of largely early eighteenth-century streets hereabouts built on land bequeathed by successful City men either to Rugby School or to

Bedford City Corporation in the sixteenth century. The building up of the area was begun by the notorious developer Nicholas Barbon at the end of the following century. It is difficult to know exactly which houses were built by this rogue – as sharp and unscrupulous as any of his modern successors – but certainly some in Bedford Row to the south of Theobalds Road and some in the central part of **Lamb's Conduit Street** on the Rugby estate.

It is a delight to stroll through these, along Rugby Street, Great Ormond Street, and those to the west of Lamb's Conduit Street, admiring, for instance, the variety of carved brackets supporting the door hoods. Number 23/24 Great James Street also sports a phoenix rising from the flames above its front door, while number 64 Lamb's Conduit Street has a nineteenth-century carving of some fasces being bound together with cords held by four hands. The 'conduit' was a system to supply water from springs hereabouts down to Holborn Cross, first installed in 1577. Number 13 Rugby Street (formerly French's Dairy and with a good tiled facade) has another such, the **White Conduit**, starting below it. During the Middle Ages, this supplied the Franciscan Greyfriars in Newgate Street in the City. After the Dissolution of the Monasteries Christ's Hospital took over from the friars.

If all this talk of water has brought on a thirst, walk to **The Lamb** almost at the northern end of Lamb's Conduit Street, a genuine neighbourhood pub and one of the few to have preserved its odd little snob screens, from the days a hundred years ago when it was first fitted out. Beyond it is a fountain in the form of a kneeling girl pouring water from a jug, and beyond that, on the far side of Guilford Street, a classical niche rescued from the demolition of the Foundling Hospital, said to be where the mothers placed their babies.

Back now to **Great Ormond Street.** Number 45 was where Lord Chancellor Thurlow was living in 1784, when the Great Seal was stolen from his house, probably by Whig supporters of the Fox-North coalition ministry attempting, unsuccessfully, to delay the dissolution of Parliament. From 1857 it and number 44 housed the Working Men's College which had been founded by the Christian Socialist F. D. Maurice a few years before, on his expulsion from King's College in the Strand for casting doubt on the doctrines of hell-fire and eternal damnation. Thomas Hughes, the author of *Tom Brown's Schooldays*, was later its Principal. The **Hospital for Sick Children** was founded in 1891 in a house where Dr Mead (p. 24) had once lived. It is well worth going in and following the signs to its byzantine jewel box of a chapel. Its floor is of mosaic and tiles; the altar rail and columns are of marble and alabaster; the walls are lined with marble where they are not covered with paintings; the starred ceiling has the symbols of the four Evangelists while a pelican-in-its-piety nests in the dome, serenaded by angels on various musical instruments. Notice in particular the child-sized pews and the gilded capitals carved with dragons, a bat, an owl, lions and squirrels.

Hospitals come thick and fast round **Queen Square**: the Italian Hospital, complete with duomo, at the south end; the Royal London Homeopathic and the National (neurological) on the east side. The latter, with its baroque terracotta porch, is on the site of the building where William Morris lived and which also housed his decorating company, 'The Firm', from 1869 until 1881. His beliefs about craftsmanship, and the importance of maintaining it in an age increasingly dominated by machines, did not leave the square for long, because the Art Worker's Guild moved into number 6 in 1914. Since 1884 like-minded craftsmen – all called brother – have met fortnightly to hear a lecture, eat bloater paste sandwiches and recapture the ideals and philosophy of the Arts and Crafts Movement.

The church of **St George the Martyr** in the south-west corner of the square began as a chapel of ease attached to St Andrew, Holborn in the 1700s, when the square was laid out, but was soon turned into a proper parish. It bears little resemblance to its original appearance, having undergone heavy restoration in 1869 and again in 1952. The uncomfortable-looking spire presumably we owe to the 'rogue Goth' architect S. S. Teulon who masterminded the first restoration. In 1834 Captain James Smith left £1000 to the church to provide an annual Christmas dinner for 1000 apprentice chimney sweeps. Each boy got ½ lb of roast or boiled beef, ½ lb of potatoes, ½ lb of plum pudding, half a loaf of bread, half a pint of ale, and a new shilling.

Before leaving the square, spare a glance for the few remaining

Sicilian Avenue – a one-off Edwardian extravaganza

Kingsway Tram Subway

eighteenth-century houses on its west side, and for the statue of a queen at the northern end of its garden. This was erected in 1775 and, on that ground alone, it is said to be of George III's consort, Queen Charlotte. Its looks are no help towards identification. Queen Charlotte has another connection here via **The Queen's Larder** pub on the corner of Cosmo Place, by the church. She is reputed to have rented its cellars and stored food there, so she could supply her poor husband with treats when he had one of his bouts of madness and was in the care of Dr Willis who lived in the square.

Go southwards from the square down **Old Gloucester Street**, past the house where Bishop Richard Challoner died in 1781. By virtue of his position as Vicar Apostolic of the London District, he was the leading figure among English Roman Catholics and, since the anti-Catholic Gordon Riots had taken place only the year before, it is hardly surprising that number 44 is so modest and retired. Continue southwards down Southampton Row, looking into **Sicilian Avenue** on the right, behind its columned screen. Constructed in 1905 out of cream terracotta that looks like processed cheese, and the smoothest of bricks with the thinnest of pointing between them, its windows a mass of bows and oriels, with turrets above and hanging baskets between, the whole thing is a slightly surreal confection. But among its businesses is a second-hand bookshop with the delightful name 'Skoob'.

In the centre of the road here is the ramp leading down to the **Kingsway Tram Subway**, opened 1906, closed 1952, biding its time for transport fashions to come full circle. Indeed, the tram lines are still visible here. Beyond it, on the east side, the 1900s sandstone Carlisle House and, more particularly, Portland stone Baptist Church House with its statue of Bunyan are worth attention. The latter has an interesting tower paying more than a little homage to Hawksmoor. By now you are outside Holborn tube, the end of this walk.

WALK TWO

Central Bloomsbury and the British Museum

Start at Holborn tube station, heading west for a short distance along High Holborn. Pretty soon the **Princess Louise** pub will appear on the left. Find an excuse to go in and admire its elaborate turn-of-the-century interior: mirrors etched with butterflies, dragonflies and birds, and superadded gilt; vertical strips of tiles, with pomegranates on them in relief; tilework panels of urns full of fruit; an arabesqued plaster ceiling and, at the foot of the stairs, a stained-glass window featuring the masks of comedy and tragedy. The beers it serves sound exotic too: Bombardier, Titanic Lifeboat, Moles Brew, Blackawton Headstrong. The branch of the Royal Bank of Scotland opposite, numbers **127–129 High Holborn**, is a fine piece of angular puritan Baroque (1904), by Charles Holden, once you get above the usual nasty blue fascia. It is to be compared with his Zimbabwe House in the Strand and Law Society extension in Chancery Lane, also from the 1900s, rather than his London University Senate House (p. 50) from the 1930s.

Turn right up **Southampton Place**, two well preserved rows of mid eighteenth-century houses, their front doors flanked by Tuscan columns and crowned by pediments. In this area such handsome streets always seem colonised by lawyers, and Southampton Place is no exception. Number 17 was the boyhood home of **John Henry Newman**, Cardinal and perhaps soon to be a saint. His father was a private banker, doing sufficiently well to move here from the City in 1802, but in 1816, in the recession following the Napoleonic War, Ramsbottom, Newman and Ramsbottom failed and the family had to leave. Go through the archway halfway up on the left into **Barter Street**, so named because it was originally built as a market to serve the wants of

St George's, Bloomsbury

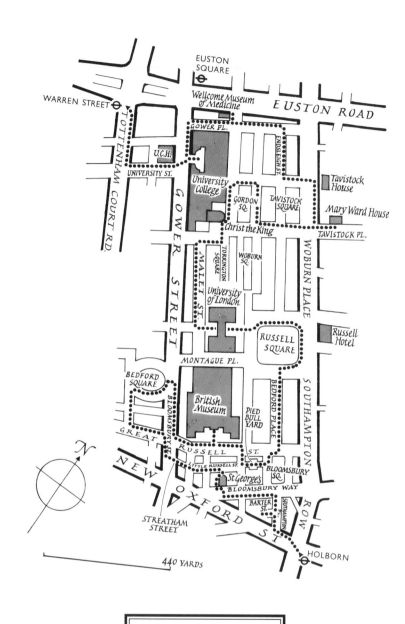

EUSTON SQUARE

WARREN STREET

EUSTON ROAD

Wellcome Museum of Medicine

GOWER PL.

ENDSLEIGH ST.

U.C.H.

UNIVERSITY ST.

University College

TOTTENHAM COURT RD.

GOWER STREET

Tavistock House

Mary Ward House

GORDON SQ.

TAVISTOCK SQUARE

Christ the King

TAVISTOCK PL.

MALET ST.

TORRINGTON SQUARE

WOBURN SQ.

WOBURN PLACE

University of London

RUSSELL SQUARE

Russell Hotel

MONTAGUE PL.

BEDFORD SQUARE

British Museum

BEDFORD PLACE

SOUTHAMPTON ROW

PIED BULL YARD

BLOOMSBURY ST.

GREAT RUSSELL ST.

LITTLE RUSSELL ST.

BLOOMSBURY SQ.

St. George's

BLOOMSBURY WAY

NEW OXFORD ST.

STREATHAM STREET

BARTER ST.

SOUTHAMPTON ROW

HOLBORN

N

440 YARDS

smart Bloomsbury Square to the north. Having glanced at some pleasant nineteenth-century shop-fronts, continue up Southampton Place to Bloomsbury Square.

Something must be said at this point about the **BLOOMSBURY ESTATE** in general. In the Middle Ages it belonged to the Carthusian monks of the Charterhouse, some distance to the east. After the Dissolution it was given to Thomas Wriothesley, Earl of Southampton, in 1550. In 1642 the 4th Earl built Southampton House and Bloomsbury Square was later laid out as a suitable architectural setting for it to the south. This was the first true London Square, with a garden at its centre, rather than Covent Garden's paved piazza of thirty years earlier. It immediately became very fashionable and attracted other magnates to the area including the Duke of Montagu, married to the Earl's sister. His house on Great Russell Street was to become the British Museum in the 1750s. The Tufton family, Earls of Thanet, had a house a little further west, which still exists as 99–106 Great Russell Street, though much altered. Southampton's heir was his daughter Rachel, and she brought the estate into the family of the Earls (then Dukes) of Bedford by her marriage to Lord William Russell. (For the story of his execution in 1683, see the Inns of Court guide in this series, p. 39. For the later history of the Bloomsbury Estate, see p. 40 below.)

Back to **Bloomsbury Square**, where none of the original seventeenth-century houses survives. Number 45, an eighteenth-century house on the north-east corner of Southampton Place, was the London home of the Stanhope family, Earls of Chesterfield. The 4th Earl is the one made notorious by some letters he sent and one he received: his own were to instruct his illegitimate son in the rules of deportment in Society. He was trenchant on the subject of sex: 'the expense is damnable, the pleasure momentary and the position ludicrous.' However, he once rather oddly defined a gentleman as someone who knows how to play a trumpet, but refrains from doing so. Some of the advice which he sent his son often seems equally bizarre: 'A man of parts and fashion is only seen to smile, but never heard to laugh.' When discussing the management of time, he commended someone who bought a common edition of Horace, tore out two sheets a day, 'carried them with him to that necessary place, read them first, and then sent them down as a sacrifice to Cloacina.'

The famous letter sent to him came from Samuel Johnson in 1754 and is one of the most thundering rebukes ever recorded, prompted by what Johnson regarded as the shabby treatment he had received from the Earl, nominally his patron during the seven years it took him to compile his great English dictionary. Modern research shows, however, that it was a case of Johnson taking umbrage when it wasn't on offer – something he was prone to do. One might have doubts about continuing to quote unjust accusations if the Earl himself were not on record as saying the letter showed the 'great powers' of Johnson, so here is one sentence. 'The notice which you have been pleased to take of my labours, had it been early, had been kind; but it has been delayed until I am indifferent, and cannot enjoy it; till I am solitary, and cannot impart it; till I am known, and do not want it.' Number 43, just beyond Lord Chesterfield's house has a good rococo plaster ceiling, visible through its ground-floor windows.

Numbers 2 and 3 Bloomsbury Square, on the other corner of Southampton Place, are the former premises of the College of Preceptors (now near Epping), one of the innumerable professional bodies spawned in the nineteenth century. It was formed as a society of teachers in 1846, to see they were properly trained and qualified, and later ran examinations for secondary schools too. As seems almost inevitable with such late-Victorian institutional buildings, it is decorated with busts of distinguished figures in its particular field: Locke, Milton, Arnold, Pestalozzi and Froebel. Just to the north, across Bloomsbury Way, number 6 was the home of Isaac Disraeli, a man of letters of independent means, author of *Curiosities of Literature*, *Calamities of Authors* and *Quarrels of Authors*, all well worth dipping into. He moved here, to be handy for the British Museum, in 1817 from a house in Theobalds Road at the southern end of John Street (p. 25), the same year in which he finally broke with the Bevis Marks Synagogue and had his children christened, including Benjamin the future Prime Minister.

Bloomsbury Square was the scene of two riots in the eighteenth century. The 4th Duke came under attack in 1765 in Bedford House from Spitalfields silk weavers, for opposing an increase of duty on imported silk. The magistrate in charge of the party of Horse Guards sent to disperse them was Saunders Welch, an intrepid thief-taker, as shown by the anecdote about him in the Covent Garden guide in this series; he was also Mrs Nollekens' father (p. 71). In 1780 Lord Mansfield, the Lord Chief Justice, had his house, number 29, burnt by the Gordon Rioters. Lord Chancellor Thurlow's house in Great Ormond Street (p. 26) escaped the same fate because a detachment of soldiers was posted to guard it. Lord Mansfield had a similar guard, but they were concealed in St George's Church to the west so as not to be provocative. Retribution in the aftermath of the riot was brutal, as Dickens described in *Barnaby Rudge*.

Two cripples – both were boys – one with a leg of wood, one who dragged his twisted limbs along with the help of a crutch, were hanged in Bloomsbury Square. As the cart was about to glide from under them, it was observed that they stood with their faces from, not to, the house they had assisted to despoil; and their misery was protracted that this omission might be remedied.

Go westwards now, along Bloomsbury Way, to the church of **ST GEORGE'S, BLOOMSBURY**. In 1710 the Tories, the party, above all else, of the Church of England, came to power, and the following year passed an act for the building of fifty new churches, to be paid for by a tax on coal. The idea was that these should be located in the new suburbs and take pressure off the old medieval parishes. St George's was one of the new churches, begun in 1716 and finished in 1731, and designed by Nicholas Hawksmoor, an architect whose star is very much in the ascendant at present.

Recent research has suggested that Hawksmoor's inspiration, particularly for his London churches further east, derived in part from his fascination with various attempts at recreating classical temples published in the previous two centuries. This explains many unexpected features in the churches, and the absence of conventional porticos and columns. Now St George's has a noble portico, and columns enough for any man, inside and out, but it also sports one of the most bizarre towers in London. It is a stepped pyramid perched on top of a mini-temple (which echoes the south front of the church below). This pyramid is derived from a description by the Roman author Pliny of the elaborate, fourth-century BC temple-tomb in Asia Minor (Turkey) known as the Mausoleum of Halicarnassus (near Bodrum), one of the Seven Wonders of the World. Whatever the comparative conventionality of the body of the church, it seems that here Hawksmoor had to indulge his fixation. Ironically much of the sculpture from the Mausoleum was brought back in the mid-nineteenth century to the British Museum, where it can be seen in Room 12. The final cherry on the cake, as it were, is the statue of King George I, in a Roman kilt, on top of the pyramid, with a lightning conductor emerging from his head. There used to be stone lions prowling down and unicorns prancing up the pyramid's four corners, contesting for crowns between them, but these had to go when they became unsafe in the last century. These accretions transformed the original Tory intentions behind the new churches, turning St George's into a brazen piece of Whig propaganda for the Hanoverians. Given its starting date, two years after the death of the last Stuart, Queen Anne, and one year after the first Jacobite uprising under the Old Pretender, this is perhaps not so surprising. The statue was paid for by William Hucks, brewer to the royal household.

St George's site was always cramped and Hawksmoor had to exercise considerable ingenuity to make the most of it. The central area is a square, once one has emerged from under the gallery, with the tower off to the left (west), the present chancel off to the north, and an east apse to the right. But the altar is not where Hawksmoor put it – in the east apse – and the second northern gallery he provided for the Duke of Montagu, matching the Duke of Bedford's southern gallery, has gone. The splendid reredos, now to the north, was in the apse until the 1780s. That still has good, gilded plasterwork against a light blue background – winged cherubs' heads, a pelican, crossed crosiers with mitres above – allowing one for a moment to imagine a scene-change to some prince-bishop's palace chapel in south Germany. A sense of theatre is encouraged by Hawksmoor's repeated use of proscenium arches here.

Underneath the tower there is a good early nineteenth-century monument (by S. Manning) to Charles Grant, MP for Inverness,

*St George's, Blooms-
bury, interior facing
north, and one of
Hawksmoor's giant
keystones on the west
side of the exterior*

Bloomsbury Way – this late flourish of classicism is scheduled for demolition

Little Russell Street, in the courtyard of the Dairy

Chairman of the East India Company, and member of the evangelical Clapham Sect, who was also instrumental in the establishment of Sierra Leone as a colony for freed slaves, and of the Church Missionary Society. He died in 1823 and the EIC erected it 'as an enduring memorial of the principles which they desire to render prevalent in the administration of the immense dominions which it has pleased Providence to confide to their charge'. Grant is seen, an expiring figure, dressed in breeches, quill in hand, sitting on an elegant Hepplewhite or Sheraton chair, Faith with a cross standing behind and a turbanned putto to the right.

After leaving the church go down the narrow alley squeezed between its west side and the vestry, so that you can enjoy a number of those giant keystones so typical of Hawksmoor. Eventually, you will also be rewarded by a sight of the north front, quite different in treatment from the south, and made up out of two orders, blank arches and arched windows.

Walk westwards along **Little Russell Street**, crossing **Museum Street**, full of second-hand and antiquarian book-shops and print sellers. At number 40, Ruskin House, the good Tyrolean-style wrought-iron sign, designed by Ruskin for his and the hobbits' publishers George Allen and Unwin, still hangs, although the firm was absorbed by another some years ago. The blank ovals with sprays draped either side, at first floor level, which decorate the houses hereabouts, are a surprisingly delicate touch for the middle years of the last century. On the corner of Little Russell Street and **Coptic Street** there are the former premises of the Dairy Supply Co. Ltd, with giant arches at the ground floor level, tilework, stylized cut-brick sunflowers, monograms and a milk churn. Little Russell Street then becomes **Streatham Street** where London's earliest block of model dwellings survives, erected in 1849 to provide decent flats, each with its own lavatory, for former slum dwellers. With its open balconies at the back, the block was the model for many such, though it has a quality to it lacking from many Peabody developments, for example.

Go right for a very short distance up Bloomsbury Street, before turning left, between the two, domed hotels – Marlborough and Kenilworth – into **Great Russell Street**. Outside **Congress House**, the headquarters of the TUC on the left, there is a clumsy statue of one man assisting another, by Bernard Meadows; in the courtyard there is another by Jacob Epstein. This war memorial would stand more of a chance if its surroundings were less oppressive. Beyond it is the YWCA building by Sir Edwin Lutyens (1932), a rather bland Wrenissance effort, redeemed by the good wrought-iron railings, and with his typical inverted obelisks either side of the window above the elaborate front-door surround. Opposite is the shop of L. Cornellisen & Son, Artists' Colourmen, a fascinating accumulation of everything for the painter and gilder. Also, behind the facades of numbers 99 to 106, there are the remains of Thanet House (p. 33).

Turn right up Adeline Place, by the hideous YMCA building, which replaced its exuberant Edwardian Baroque predecessor in the 1970s. You will shortly emerge in Bedford Square, one of the most handsome left in London, and always a 'good address'. In *Sketches by Boz*, Dickens included a short story entitled 'The Bloomsbury Christening'. It contains a character who is something of a dry run for Scrooge, Mr Nicodemus Dumps; he is 'afflicted with a situation in the Bank worth £500 a year' and uncle to Mr Charles Kitterbell of 14 Great Russell Street, Bedford Square, father of the baby to be christened at St George's (a plaque marks the Kitterbell house opposite the YMCA). Dickens added that, in order to puncture his nephew's pretensions, 'Uncle Dumps always dropped the "Bedford Square" and inserted in lieu thereof the dreadful words "Tottenham Court Road".'

Bedford Square was built by Gertrude Leveson-Gower, widow of the Duke whom the silk weavers had attacked, during the minority of her grandson, the 5th Duke. It represents the start of the second phase of the development of its Bloomsbury estate by the Russell family, and was followed through the first half of the nineteenth century by Russell, Tavistock, Torrington, Woburn and Gordon Squares, together with their linking streets.

In spite of wartime bombing and the more serious damage inflicted by the cuckoo-like expansion of London University, there is still some unity and a residual seemliness and dignity to the area, created not by individual buildings but by the rhythm of the stucco and brick terraces, and the refreshment of the green plane trees as the streets open out into the squares. The Bedford Estate cultivated these qualities from the start by the restrictions it put on first its builders and then its tenants, through a system of restrictive covenants and carefully timed leases, which prevented structural alterations or changes of use. Until the 1890s entry and egress to and from the squares was controlled by gates, to stop disturbance from through traffic, and local tradesmen were forced to deliver goods themselves rather than sending errand boys.

James Burton, the first of the nineteenth-century builders associated with the estate, has already been encountered on p. 16, as has his successor **Thomas Cubitt**. The latter took over from the former around 1820, completing Tavistock Square, then Woburn Place and part of Gordon Square. Gordon Street, Endsleigh Street and Endsleigh Place were also his. A third builder, James Sim, was responsible for Torrington and Woburn Squares.

Bloomsbury was far from being Thomas Cubitt's only sphere of operation: he was also creating Belgravia and Pimlico. As the nineteenth century advanced, these areas to the west, together with Kensington and 'Tyburnia' to the north of the Bayswater Road, became the fashionable neighbourhoods, so much closer to the green lungs of Kensington Gardens and Hyde Park, as well as the shops of Bond Street and the gentlemen's clubs of Pall Mall. Bloomsbury increasingly became the preserve of professionals – lawyers who wanted to be close to the Inns of Court, medical men, architects.

Bedford Square achieves its effect with quite simple ingredients: each doorway has a bearded-head keystone above it and intermittent vermiculated rustication around it, all made from that mysterious artificial substance, Coade Stone. At the centre of each side two houses are pedimented and pilastered. The central garden is circular, which adds to the suavity of the whole.

From 1786 until his death in 1810 the brilliant but reclusive scientist **Henry Cavendish** lived at number 11. A grandson of the 2nd Duke of Devonshire, perhaps his greatest achievement was to discover the ingredients of water, H_2O. He was morbidly shy and had a shrill voice when he did speak. Lord Brougham said, 'he possibly uttered fewer words in the course of his life than any man who ever lived to fourscore years, not at all excepting the monks of La Trappe.' He died leaving a fortune of over £1 million.

Bedford Square, south-west corner

Bedford Square, bikes and vermiculated rustication outide the Architectural Association

A ladies college opened at number 11 in 1849, then as Bedford College became part of London University in 1880, and moved to Regent's Park in 1913, before amalgamating with the Royal Holloway College in Egham a few years ago. The Architectural Association is on the west side of the square and the Publishers' Association on the north, though the many publishers who used to congregate here have all moved out.

Back southwards down Bloomsbury Street then left into the other half of Great Russell Street so as to reach the **BRITISH MUSEUM**. It has recently been granted £30m of National Lottery money to help pay for the major changes which will be triggered when the British Library removes itself to the Euston Road (p. 12). And it was with the help of a state lottery that it began life in the 1750s, when money was raised, first to buy the collection of Sir Hans Sloane, the most fashionable doctor of his day, and then to place it, with various other accumulations, in Montagu House. Soane's massive hoard was a mixture of natural history and antiquities, but the other foundation collections of the BM were the manuscripts assembled by Sir Robert Cotton (d. 1631) and by Robert and Edward Harley, successive Earls of Oxford, early in the eighteenth century. It is to Cotton that we owe the Lindisfarne Gospels, the manuscript of *Beowulf*, and two copies of Magna Carta. The old Royal Library, started by Edward IV in about 1471, soon joined them, bringing with it the right to a copy of every book published in the country. This is a blessing which seems increasingly mixed as the new volumes look set rapidly to outrun even the huge amount of extra shelving at Euston Road.

The museum's doors opened in 1759 on three days a week, guarded by armed sentries, a security measure only dropped in 1863; daily opening started in 1879. In 1762 George III gave a collection of seventeenth-century pamphlets called the Thomason Tracts; in 1772 the British ambassador in Naples, Sir William Hamilton (the future husband of Nelson's Emma), sold the collection of Greek vases he had collected from sites in southern Italy; 1802 saw the arrival of the Egyptian antiquities, including the Rosetta Stone, assembled by the French army there and captured by the British after their victory at Alexandria; in 1805 the Greek and Roman marbles collected by Charles Towneley were bought.

They include a marble vase regarded as the most likely inspiration for Keats' 'Ode on a Grecian Urn':

> What men or gods are these? What maidens loath?
> What mad pursuit? What struggle to escape?
> What pipes and timbrels? What wild ecstasy?

But in 1815–16 these were eclipsed by the arrival of the Elgin Marbles from the Parthenon in Athens and those from the Temple of Apollo at Bassae. As the century progressed, attention gradually shifted eastwards, from the Classical world to Assyria and Persia, and the winged bulls and reliefs brought back from the palaces of Nimrud and Nineveh; or to the treasures rescued from the lost cities and caves along the Silk Road in central Asia. And all the time coins, manuscripts, books, prints, drawings, and ethnic artefacts from seemingly every tribe under the sun flowed in, quickly filling up the space created by the removal of the Natural History collection to South Kensington in 1880.

The British Museum is the largest Classical building in the British Isles, as one might guess when confronted by the forty-four massive Ionic columns of Robert Smirke's south front. Smirke's replacement for old Montagu House was begun in 1823, but this south range was only completed in 1847. As also the world's greatest accumulation of archaeological finds, it is very fitting that the museum should be housed in a Greek Revival building. That style, aiming at primitive archaic purity, owed its very existence to the pioneer archaeologists working round the Mediterranean in the eighteenth century. When a young man, Smirke followed in their footsteps, like Inwood of St Pancras Church (p. 15), passing through Napoleonic Paris disguised as an American before travelling extensively in Greece.

If you feel rather crushed and overawed by the portico, glance upward at Richard Westmacott's heavily symbolic statuary in the pediment above ('Man emerging from savagery through the influence of Religion'), and enjoy the toothy crocodile lurking at the extreme west end, balanced by a turtle at the east end. Then take a deep breath and, like 6½ million others each year, plunge in to the entrance hall, pick up a free floor plan and turn left through the bookshop. This will position you strategically for the big Assyrian, Egyptian or Classical pieces: you can muse like Shelley in 'Ozymandias' on the 'sneers of cold command' among the Egyptian sculpture or, like Keats, suffer the 'dizzy pain' caused by the mingling of 'Grecian grandeur with the rude wasting of old time' in the Elgin Marbles room. But also spare five minutes to look at the frieze of fighting Greeks and Amazons, Centaurs and Lapiths brought back from the Temple of Apollo at Bassae. Smirke had visited the site, but it was his friend C. R. Cockerell (son of S. P. – see p. 21) who later spotted one of the marbles down a fox-hole. (Members of the Travellers' Club in Pall Mall can give the frieze a miss because a cast of it decorates the library there.) Close to it in Room 7 is the Nereid Monument from Xanthos – the young girls in wind-blown draperies are ravishing, headless though they be. The basement floor here is probably not for your first visit, but one day do go down to look at the Townley collection, and judge for yourself whether it deserves such demotion. When down there, also stray into Room 77. It is like the ultimate architectural salvage yard, or a builder's depot belonging to the gods, full of offcuts from architraves and cornices, capitals and column drums.

Back to the main hall, via the Assyrian Lion Hunt reliefs in Room 17. You cannot go straight ahead in the hall because that leads to the book stacks and the Reading Room, built in the central quadrangle of the museum in the 1850s and sporting Robert Smirke's younger brother Sydney's cast-iron ribbed dome that outdoes both St Peter's and St Paul's. A reader's ticket is required to penetrate to this, the Nation's cranium, and sit there (at O7 where Marx sat or L13 where Lenin sat), as Virginia Woolf put it, 'as if one were a thought in the huge bold forehead' of the dome. Sadly, this particular line of imagery will cease to be apposite when the British Library relocates, but the Reading Room will then be thrown open to everyone as part of the BM's Millenium-cum-250th Anniversary plan. Norman Foster is to roof in the whole of the quadrangle with steel and glass; underneath balconies will be thrown out from the sides of the Reading Room, as well as bridges linking it with the upper galleries of the BM. Some of the space resulting from the departure of the books will house the ethnographical collections, which will come back from the Museum of

Mankind in Burlington Gardens where they have been since 1970.

Until this massive reshuffle is complete, unless you want to see smaller antiquities or the Medieval, Renaissance and Modern collections, or your morbid children have an urge to see some shrivelled mummies (in which case go up the main stairs), it is best to go right. You can pore over cases of illuminated or literary manuscripts and then walk through the King's Library, the BM's best interior, housing George III's library, 'given' to the BM by George IV, in return for £180,000. At its far end is the Mexican Gallery, a spectacular vanguard for the ethnographic collection. Morbid children will also find a close examination of the Mayan reliefs there well repaid. Up the short flight of stairs, along the passage, and one emerges into the brilliant new China, South and Southeast Asia Gallery. If you leave this at its mid-point, which divides China from India and the rest, there is a lift which will take you up to the elegant Japanese galleries on Level 5. Do not miss the wall cabinets as you leave the lift, full of miraculous *netsuke*, *inro* and sword fittings. The lift will also take you down to Level 1 where the Islamic Gallery is by the door out to the north front. This was completed in 1914 by Sir John Burnet who paid a graceful compliment to Smirke's portico by also using Ionic columns, though here they are attached. The lions on either side of the door, by Albert Hemstock Hodge, must have the most supercilious expressions of any in London.

Back to the south front, using your plan-reading skills to the full to work out a variant route. Ponder as you go the thought that only 45,000 out of the BM's total collection of seven million objects are on show at any time, while the rest are in store, some in the basements, guarded by a breed of semi-feral albino cats. Or, if you prefer, dwell on the impoverished Frederick Rolfe, Baron Corvo, author of *Hadrian VII*, bathing illicitly in the cloakroom.

The whole area to the south of the south front railings, down to St George's, was to have been razed to the ground in the 1960s to make room for the expansion of the Museum and Library, but that particular bit of grandiosity never came to pass. So you can turn to the left along Great Russell Street before turning right into Bury Place for **Pied Bull Yard** and **Galen Place** off it. These two 'refurbished' courtyards house a number of shops selling antique and second-hand cameras and photography equipment. There is an elaborate clock outside the former, with a number of whimsical figures, including a bull, which no doubt can be seen pursuing each other at the right times.

Emerge into the north-west end of **Bloomsbury Square** by the German Historical Institute in what was the Pharmaceutical Society's premises, by the young John Nash (1783) and the first of his buildings to be stuccoed. Cross the road to the Square garden so you can examine Westmacott's statue of **Charles James Fox**, greatest of the Whigs, gambler on a heroic scale, sworn foe of George III, champion of the anti-slavery cause – and something of a father-figure to the orphaned 5th Duke of Bedford up to whose statue he gazes in Russell Square to the north. Shaded by a fig tree, Fox is seated, dressed in a toga, with a scroll propped on his right knee. On closer examination this turns out to be Magna Carta, with the seal of King John attached. The statue was paid for with the money left over from Westmacott's monument to Fox at the west end of Westminister Abbey.

The whole of the east side of the square is taken up by the bulk of the Liverpool and Victoria Friendly Society's premises. Bedford House, previously Southampton House, on the north side, was demolished in 1800 and a terrace of houses by James Burton (p. 16) stands in its place. Go north up **Bedford Place** until you stand under the statue of the 5th Duke of Bedford in **Russell Square**, again by Westmacott. Like the Earl of Chesterfield at the hands of Dr Johnson (p. 34), the Duke was the subject of a devastating reprimand, in his case from Edmund Burke in his *Letter to a Noble Lord* (1796). The Duke had been unwise enough to attack Burke for accepting a pension from the Crown:

I was not, like his Grace of Bedford, swaddled and rocked, and dandled into a legislator . . . At every step of my progress in life . . . I was obliged to show my passport . . . Everything of him and about him is from the throne. Is it for *him* to question the dispensation of royal favour?

The Duke never married, though when on the Grand Tour he lived in a *ménage à trois* with Lord and Lady Maynard. This showed little originality: she had already been the mistress of the Dukes of Dorset and Grafton before marrying Maynard. When the Duke

An eagle-headed protective spirit from King Ashurnasirpal's palace of Nimrud, Assyria. Now in the British Museum

An entrance hard to miss: the Hotel Russell

gave up politics he took up agriculture instead, holding the famous annual Woburn Sheep Shearings lasting five days each June. These were in emulation of Coke of Norfolk's similar events at Holkham, where tenant farmers and other enthusiasts were shown and discussed the latest agricultural developments. The statue echoes this side of the Duke: he rests one hand on a plough while in the other he holds some ears of wheat. There are putti with cornucopiae, a sheep, bulls' heads on the corners, and two panels depicting idealized agriculture.

The doorways and windows of the south and north sides of the square have terracotta trim, added in the late nineteenth century, almost as if they had caught an infection of the material from the **Hotel Russell** (1898) on the north-east side. It is a wonderful terracotta extravaganza by C. FitzRoy Doll and to the south there used to be a companion hotel, the Imperial, even more buccaneering in its approach to styles, also by Doll. Pevsner called it 'a much more vicious mixture of Art Nouveau Gothic and Art Nouveau Tudor.' Alas the Imperial was demolished in the 1960s and all that remains is a notice directing you to its phantom Turkish baths, let into the pavement at the junction of Guilford Street with the square. Doll was surveyor to the Bloomsbury Estate and served more than one term as mayor of Holborn, so it is unsurprising that he could build exactly what he liked.

Whatever one calls the Hotel Russell's style – Flemish Renaissance with Tudor touches, perhaps – there is much pleasure to be got from its details. At the ground-floor level, the squat, fluted columns have putti cavorting round their bases, while there are sleeping cupids at the foot of the Art Nouveau lamp standards punctuating the railings. The first floor has the coats of arms of various dynasties and countries – the Turkish crescent, the Japanese chrysanthemum; the Hapsburg, Hohenzollern and Romanov eagles; the lion of Holland. The fourth floor has good grotesque faces, while the coat of arms and supporters of the Russell family feature in cartouches both on the north side and flanking the main entrance. This has a bravura lion-and-unicorn and royal coat of arms above it, together with statues of four British queens. Finally, the south side has four very bad terracotta busts of, at a guess, Salisbury, Gladstone, Disraeli and Palmerston.

By the north-east corner entrance to the square garden, opposite the Hotel Russell's piece of gross exploitation, 'Virginia
Woolf's', serving burgers, pasta, grills, there is an extraordinary
clutter of street furniture – black cubes to hold paper for recycling
and clothes for Oxfam; wheeled bottle banks for brown, green
(Hock, Moselle?), plain glass, and tins; four new phone kiosks; two
different models of automatic toilet, one high-tech and the other
with post-modern gilt bands and knobs. There is also a vandalised
fountain on a scruffy patch of grass surrounded by vandalised
low railings, littered with empty cans of Skol Superstrength and
Thunderbird bottles that haven't quite made it into the banks. It is
altogether a gruesome scene, partly caused by ecological correct-
ness swamping environmental good taste.

Turn from all this and think instead of the days when Thack-
eray placed the homes of the Sedleys and the Osbornes here in
Vanity Fair; of the boy Dickens walking through it on the way to
work at the notorious blacking factory, 'with some cold hotch-
potch in a small basin tied up in a handkerchief', or even of the
early days of the publishers Faber & Faber at number 24, when the
deranged first wife of T. S. Eliot, one of their directors, poured a
tureen of hot chocolate through the letter box. From the west side
of the Square you can walk through to the University of London's
Senate House and Library built in 1933 on a site created by the
clearing away of some redundant mews and paid for in part by
£400,000 which Lord Beveridge managed to obtain from the
Rockefeller Foundation. In the Second World War it was com-
mandeered for the Ministry of Information and, indeed, George
Orwell took it as his model for the Ministry of Truth in *1984*. There
is something of a modernist-totalitarian tendency to its blocks.
Charles Holden (p. 31), its architect, built excellent underground
stations at this period, but here his touch seems rather to have
deserted him. There was, however, a lot of sculptural detail in his
designs that was never added. The hallway, through which you
should walk to get to Malet Street, shows Holden back on form.
On the west side of Malet Street, at its junction with Keppel
Street, there's the **London School of Tropical Medicine**. Its
first-floor metal balconies are decorated with giant gilded mos-
quitoes, fleas, flies, cobras and rats: perhaps a recognition of just

Frenetic terracotta:
Dillon's University Bookshop,
Torrington Place

A cool contrast:
London University
Senate House, hallway

how doughty some of its foes are. Turn right up Malet Street until **Dillon's University Bookshop** is reached. This is another phantasmagoria by FitzRoy Doll (1907) for the Bloomsbury Estate, hence the elements of the Russell coat of arms dotted among the encrustations, piping, gables, turrets and oriel windows. There are also gargoyles, lion masks and seated ladies with cornucopiae.

Turn right at the top of Malet Street and **Torrington Square** opens up almost immediately on the right. There are only six of its original houses left, on the east side, and in 1874 the poet **Christina Rossetti** moved to number 30, one of them. The sister of the Pre-Raphaelite Dante Gabriel Rossetti, she lived there with her mother and two aunts; they in turn were the sisters of Byron's travelling physician and butt of his cruel humour, Dr Polidori. It is a far cry from the

> Figs to fill your mouth,
> Citrons from the south

of her *Goblin Market*. Visitors to number 30 remarked on the total silence and the 'smell of ageing flesh'.

> Remember me when I am gone away,
> Gone far away into the silent land;
> When you can no more hold me by the hand,
> Nor I half turn to go yet turning stay.

Cross the road northwards into **Gordon Square** and the former University Church of **Christ the King**. This began life in 1855 as the cathedral of the **Catholic Apostolic Church**, an outlandish sect which, instead of adopting the usual strict puritanical low-church leanings of such congregations, went as high as it could in its espousal of all things Romish. Traits that distinguished its followers from the Catholics were their enthusiasm for 'glossolalia', speaking in tongues, and their belief in the imminence of the Second Coming. This latter allowed them to make no provision for replacing the original 'Apostles', as their elders were called. So successive generations of priests could not be ordained and their church was doomed to extinction. It was always a rich middle-class sect with the banker Henry Drummond as the key figure, after the death in 1834 of Edward Irving, the Scottish minister and popular preacher who was looked upon as founder. Irving was famous enough in his day to be skewered by William Hazlitt (p. 96) in his collection of biographical essays called *The Spirit of The Age* (1825):

He has, with an unlimited and daring licence, mixed the sacred and the profane together, the carnal and the spiritual man, the petulance of the bar with the dogmatism of the pulpit, the theatrical and the theological, the modern and the obsolete . . . Mr Irving keeps the public in awe by insulting their favourite idols . . . He makes war on all arts and sciences, upon the faculties and nature of man, on his vices and his virtues, on all existing institutions, and all possible improvements, that nothing may be left but the Kirk of Scotland, and that he may be head of it.

The Kirk expelled Irving shortly after. His other claim to fame was that he introduced Thomas Carlyle to his future wife, Jane Welsh, in 1821. The Church's wealth explains why it could afford to commission from Raphael Brandon what John Betjeman called, with Lancing College Chapel, 'the best examples of the pure medievalist architecture in the Pugin tradition I know.'

Its 300-foot spire and tower and the two most westerly bays of the nave never got built, but it is still vast. Betjeman said that elements from Salisbury, Lichfield, Lincoln and Carlisle Cathedrals can be detected. Above is a thirteenth-century arcade and triforium, then a fifteenth-century hammerbeam roof of East Anglian type. 'The whole is welded together by an exquisite sense of proportion.' Look out for the paired corbels on either side of the nave – lion and lamb, fish and bird, sun, moon and stars, Adam and Eve, wheat and trees – for the marvellous bosses among the rib vaulting above the choir, for the marble floor and the seven brass altar lamps hanging in a row in front of the high altar. A thin screen rising behind it separates off the east chapel, with its stencilled wooden ceiling, tiled floor, musician angels forming the lower corbels and singing angels with their mass books on the higher ones. There is something missing, over and above the usual clutter of monuments that one would expect in such a building: what it desperately needs is to be back in use, not bereft of a congregation, as it is now. If the church is locked, there is a bell for the caretaker.

Turn left outside the church, past the building next door called the 'Cloisters', with its Venetian Gothic balcony, until you come to number 14 Gordon Square. This Tudor Gothic building began life in 1849 as a hostel for Unitarian students from nearby University College, but since 1890 it has housed **Dr Williams's Library**. Daniel Williams was a Presbyterian minister who died in 1716, leaving his library of over 6000 books and the money with which to erect a building to house them, so that they could be read by anyone, without distinction. The first Library building was in Cripplegate in the City, where it remained from 1729 until 1865; for the next twenty-five years it was somewhat peripatetic, until it came to rest in Gordon Square. Many more books and manuscripts have been added to the Library over the years, including the 'scientific portion' of George Eliot's library, and it remains an outstanding source for students of theology, ecclesiastical history, philosophy, and English nonconformity in particular. Number 14 is also home to the Royal Institute of Philosophy. Look inside the entry hall, for there is a good Arts and Crafts brass chandelier above the flagged floor, and a ribbed ceiling above that. The lecture hall down the steps is also worth a look.

The architecture of Gordon Square is less uniform than that of other Squares in Bloomsbury because it was completed later (1860) and so was more susceptible to the mid-nineteenth-century property slump. Developers here kept on changing styles in an attempt to sustain interest. After their father Sir Leslie Stephen's death in 1904, Virginia Woolf, her sister Vanessa and brothers Thoby and Adrian moved from their oppressive family house in Kensington to number 46 Gordon Square, on the east side. It was a momentous step, gaining them not only more light and space, but freedom too: 'We are going to do without table napkins . . . to have coffee after dinner instead of tea at nine o'clock.' Thoby had been a member of the secretive society known as the Apostles in Cambridge, founded by F. D. Maurice (p. 26) in the 1820s. Soon other Apostles like Lytton Strachey, Leonard Woolf and Maynard Keynes were coalescing round the core of the Stephen family, and in due course the **Bloomsbury Group** emerged. If these writers and artists had any sort of sacred text, it lay within the writings of the contemporary Cambridge philosopher G. E. Moore, with

Gordon Square: the garden and Dr Williams' Library

their emphasis on the importance of friendship and of beauty.

Maynard Keynes, the brilliant economist whom Virginia Woolf likened to 'quicksilver on a sloping board', lived at number 46 from 1916 to 1946, some time after the Stephen household had broken up, while Lytton Strachey lived at number 51. In 1918 Virginia Woolf wrote, when temporarily out of the Bloomsbury swim, 'The dominion that Bloomsbury exercises over the sane and insane alike seems to be sufficient to turn the brains of the most robust . . . Maynard seems to be the chief fount of the magic spirit.' What was true then has certainly also been true of the last twenty-five years, when interest in the Group has at times seemed obsessive. Would that some of the energies poured into the study of them had been diverted into raising funds to get rid of the chain-link fence round Gordon Square and restoring its railings.

On the south-east corner of the Square, at number 53, will be found the **Percival David Foundation**, a collection of Chinese ceramics (10.30 to 5.00, closed weekends). If the thought of wandering, probably alone, through three floors of dragons, lotus blossoms and carp is to your liking, then this is the place for you. **Woburn Square**, on the south side of the road, has suffered more than most at the hands of London University. In 1958 Charles Holden built the **Warburg Institute** in the north-west corner. This powerhouse of art history began life in Hamburg in 1866, but fled to this country to escape the Nazis. It is hard to see its activities reflected in its bricks and mortar, though there is a diagrammatic Latin inscription about the Four Elements above the door. The southern end of the square went in the 1960s, including Christ Church, to make way for such gems as Denys Lasdun's Institute of Education, and the School of Oriental and African Studies.

The next square eastwards is **Tavistock Square**. The Tavistock Hotel at its southern end occupies the site of number 52, where Virginia and Leonard Woolf lived and ran the Hogarth Press from 1924 until 1939. It was here, when not at Rodmell in Sussex, that she wrote most of her books. When she moved here from Richmond she exclaimed, 'Oh the convenience of this place! and the loveliness too. We walk home from theatres, through the entrails of London.'

Cross Woburn Place at the traffic lights by the hotel and go a few yards down **Tavistock Place** to number 5, **Mary Ward House**, on the left. Now the National Institute for Social Work, this began as the Passmore Edwards Settlement, built in 1898 by Dunbar Smith and Cecil Brewer, in an Arts and Crafts style that reflected the influence of a number of fellow architects. Voysey's has been suggested as the spirit behind the cornice and roof, Townsend's (of the Horniman Museum and Whitechapel Art Gallery) behind the entrance, and Norman Shaw's behind the windows. This was a 'university settlement' where graduates were meant to reside so that they could mix with the local working class in the evenings and spread sweetness and light through lectures and conversation. The moving spirit was Mrs Humphry Ward, grand-daughter of Arnold of Rugby and a hugely successful Late-Victorian novelist. Her books, such as *Robert Elsmere*, mirrored the contemporary preoccupation with what her uncle, Matthew Arnold, in his poem 'Dover Beach', called 'the sea of faith' and 'its melancholy, long, withdrawing roar' in the face of Progress and Science. Passmore Edwards was a wealthy newspaper proprietor and Liberal M P who provided the money for this, and seventy other free libraries, hospitals and the like.

Back in Tavistock Square, the garden centrepiece is a statue of **Mahatma Gandhi**, architect of Indian independence, sitting cross-legged and usually with some cellophane-wrapped bunches of flowers in his lap. The north-east corner of the Square is occupied now by **Tavistock House**. Dickens lived in part of a predecessor from 1851 to 1860, years when he wrote *Bleak House, Little Dorrit, Hard Times, A Tale of Two Cities* and *Great Expectations.*
The present building (1938), headquarters of the British Medical Association, was designed by **Sir Edwin Lutyens** for the Theosophists, with whom his wife Emily had been deeply involved, but they never moved in. The brick pilasters and columns and the segmental pediment above the main entrance are to be admired, as are the two war memorials within the courtyard. First War medics are commemorated by an elegant wrought-iron screen and gates designed by Lutyens, while the fountain is for those who died in the Second War. Its four rounded, streamlined figures are by **James Woodford**, who carved the heraldic Queen's Beasts for the

1953 Coronation, now round the pond in Kew Gardens. They stand for Sacrifice, Cure, Prevention and Aspiration. The helmeted Greek warrior is Machaon, son of Aesculapius the God of Medicine, who died in the Trojan War. He was both surgeon and soldier, and represents Sacrifice. As well as his father's symbol of a staff entwined with snakes, his shield has the symbols of Combined Operations: the spread-eagle, the anchor and the tommy gun. Cure holds a scalpel while his two putti hold a cupping dish and a trepanning drill. Prevention is an early nineteenth-century figure clasping a microscope, while his dog and sheep refer to inoculation. Aspiration is a mother leading a child into the future.

The Jewish Museum used to be on the north side of Tavistock Square, but recently moved to Albert Street, NW1. Go north up **Endsleigh Street**, pausing to look at the Art Deco bas reliefs of workers on Bentham House at the top, before turning left along Endsleigh Gardens. A very short diversion north up Gordon Street will take you to 193 Euston Road, and the **Wellcome Museum** of medical science, a model of its kind. Otherwise continue along Gower Place before turning left into **Gower Street** where you will come to the entrance to **University College**. This was founded in 1826, to provide education for non-Anglicans excluded from Oxford and Cambridge, by a group of friends of religious toleration including Lord Chancellor Brougham, Thomas Campbell the poet, and the Utilitarians James Mill and Jeremy Bentham. The leaders of London's Jewish community were also involved, such as Nathan Meyer Rothschild, two members of the Mocatta family, and Isaac Lyon Goldsmid. His children's tutor was Thomas Campbell, and he bought the site for £30,000 at his own risk.

The original range that faces you was completed by William Wilkins, he of the National Gallery, in 1829. Go past the catalpas, ginkgos, cherries and two small domed observatories, then skirt the noble fights of stairs leading to the portico on its podium. Ever since a fire in 1836 this latter has not been the entrance because the assembly hall to which it led was burnt, and replaced by the library. Head instead for the entrance in the top-right corner of the quadrangle because this will allow you to pay your

Lutyens' war memorial gates in the courtyard of Tavistock House, home of the BMA

The Flaxman Gallery, University College

respects to the remains of **Jeremy Bentham**, what he called his
'Auto Icon' in his will. Inside a glass-fronted box is his skeleton
'put together in such a manner that the whole figure may be seated
in a chair usually occupied by me when living'. The skeleton is
dressed in Bentham's usual outfit, including a frilled shirt and
straw hat. He holds a stick and his spectacles are to hand. The face
which you see is of wax, and his mummified head actually resides
in the College safe. It is worth quoting some more of his will:

If it should so happen that my personal friends and other disciples
should be disposed to meet together on some day or days of the year for
the purpose of commemorating the founder of the greatest happiness
system of morals and legislation [Utilitarianism] my executor will from
time to time cause to be conveyed to the room in which they meet the
said box or case with the contents therein to be stationed in such a part
of the room as the assembled company shall so meet.

He was obviously determined not to miss out on a party. Now find
your way to the **Flaxman Gallery** under the central dome of the
College. John Flaxman (1755–1826) was a leading exponent of the
neo-Classical style, which owed so much to the Greek vases and
reliefs that started pouring into Britain – and the British Museum
– from the 1760s. It is no surprise to hear that he was employed by
Wedgwood, before going out to Italy and then making an interna-
tional reputation with his idiosyncratic outline drawings illustrating Dante, Homer and Aeschylus. His vision was of an ideal world,
pure and severe, and it lent itself to the funerary monuments
which formed by far the greatest part of his output as a sculptor.
The way he worked was to make a clay model that was then cast in
plaster. This acted as the guide for his assistants who actually
pointed up the marbles.

It is the casts that are gathered below the College dome, where
they have been since 1857. Even though nearly 100 were lost in the
Blitz when the dome was gutted, they still make a fine display. Note
in particular three on the south-west wall that feature Indian
figures: 'Sir William Jones forming a digest of Hindu and
Mohammedan Laws assisted by learned Pandits', a Brahmin and a
Muslim sage for Josiah Webbe's monument, and 'a Brahmin and a
Mohammedan in Earnest converse for their country's good' for

General Sir Barry Close's monument – numbers, 21, 23 and 26. On the north-west wall number 34, Ann and Elizabeth Yarborough distributing arms to the poor, and number 39, Sir Isaac Pocock dying in the arms of his niece in a boat on the Thames, are particularly effective. The large freestanding group in the middle of St Michael overcoming Satan is a cast of the original at Petworth, commissioned by the Lord Egremont who also patronized Turner. The painting above, by Henry Tonks, shows Wilkins presenting his plans for the College to Bentham.

University College is also home to the **Petrie Museum of Egyptian Archaeology** – though frankly, if you have time for only one such collection, then go for the British Museum's – and the **Slade School of Fine Art**. Perhaps its greatest moment was just before the First War. There is a group portrait taken at a picnic then, which includes David Bomberg, Isaac Rosenberg, Dora Carrington, C. R. W. Nevinson, Stanley Spencer, William Roberts and Mark Gertler.

As you come out of the quadrangle you will see the apparition that is **University College Hospital** (1897–1906), Camelot come to Bloomsbury. Alfred Waterhouse was the architect, and he used the same 'Slaughterhouse' red brick and terracotta as he employed for the Prudential Building in Holborn. The lighter shades of his Natural History Museum would have been better suited. It is cruciform in shape with Arthurian towers at each corner.

Go along University Street to Tottenham Court Road. The family that used to own the farm hereabouts in the eighteenth century were called **Capper** and their name adorns the street one to the south. There were two maiden Capper sisters: one rode about armed with shears to cut the strings of children's kites; the other specialised in carrying off the clothes of boys who bathed in their ponds and brooks. The walk ends at Warren Street tube, a little to the north.

NO 4

Begin at Goodge Street tube, halfway up the Tottenham Court Road. Tottenham Court was famous in the eighteenth century for its pubs and teahouses, such as the King's Head and the Adam and Eve, both of which can be seen in Hogarth's *March to Finchley* at the Coram Foundation (p. 22). Before setting out look across the road at **Heal's** well composed furniture store built in 1916 by Smith and Brewer (p. 57), with its octagonal columns forming a colonnade in front of the shop windows. Its vestigial pilasters above, between small-paned windows, make plain the steel stanchions of its structure. Then cross the road into Chenies Street. Here is **North Crescent**, linked to **South Crescent** by **Alfred Place**, the ensemble laid out by George Dance in the 1790s. North Crescent is encumbered by some sort of wartime bunker now used for storing security archives. This lowers over the war memorial of **The Rangers**, the 12th County of London Regiment, with a familiar litany of names on it – Ypres, Somme, Passchendaele, Western Desert.

There's nothing to detain you in Alfred Place or, indeed, in South Crescent, though it is pleasantly draped with creepers. Cross back over Tottenham Court Road to the **Rising Sun** on the corner of Windmill Street, whose exterior by **Henry Treadwell** and **Leonard Martin** (1897) is one of London's best. Their work, whether shop fronts or pubs as here, is always full of inventiveness and refinement, cross-breeding Arts and Crafts ideas with Gothic imagery and an almost Rococo flamboyance. There are splendid variants of 'green men', grotesque masks coming out of foliage, or flanked by wings, or hawks' heads. Above the main door there is a double-tailed merman, then cherubim above him, and the Lincoln Imp's younger brother at the top.

Tottenham Court Road is a horrible street in which as little time

The Rising Sun pub, Tottenham Court Road

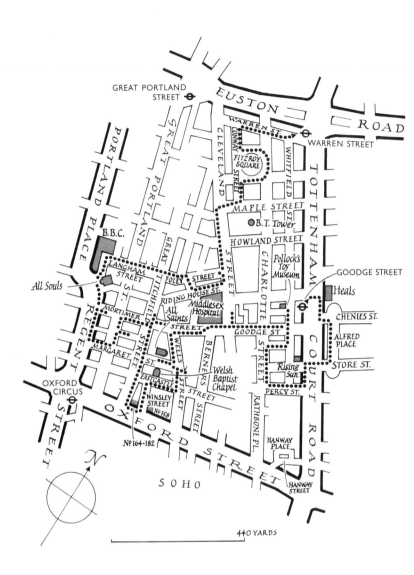

GREAT PORTLAND
STREET

EUSTON

ROAD

WARREN ST.

WARREN STREET

CLEVELAND

CONWAY

FITZROY
SQUARE

STREET

WHITFIELD

TOTTENHAM

MAPLE STREET

B.T. Tower

HOWLAND STREET

PORTLAND

PLACE

GREAT

PORTLAND

STREET

B.B.C.

CHARLOTTE

COURT

Pollock's
Toy
Museum

GOODGE STREET

LANGHAM
STREET

TITCHFIELD

FOLEY

STREET

Heals

All Souls

RIDING HOUSE ST.

STREET

CHENIES ST.

Middlesex
Hospital

ROAD

MORTIMER

ST.

All
Saints

STREET

ALFRED
PLACE

GOODGE ST.

STREET

REGENT

MARGARET

TITCHFIELD

WELLS

BERNERS

STORE ST.

OXFORD
CIRCUS

ST.

EASTCASTLE

STREET

Welsh
Baptist
Chapel

STREET

Rising
Sun

STREET

WINSLEY
STREET
Nº 158

PERCY ST.

STREET

Nº 164-182

OXFORD

STREET

RATHBONE PL.

HANWAY
PLACE

N

SOHO

HANWAY
STREET

440 YARDS

WALK THREE

as possible should be spent, so the route of this walk goes right into Percy Street, not very far south down it from the Rising Sun. However, there are two half-forgotten alleys in the northern elbow formed by Oxford Street and Tottenham Court Road: **Hanway Street** and **Hanway Place**. They have bags of atmosphere, little architectural merit and a number of specialist shops for collectors of old rock, pop and jazz recordings, with names like Vinyl Experience and On The Beat. **William Godwin**, the early anarchist and father of Mary Shelley, ran a children's bookshop in Hanway Street in the 1800s, with his second wife, the mother of Claire Clairmont, one of Byron's conquests. He also wrote a number of pioneering children's books, publishing them, and more by other authors, from here. Charles and Mary Lamb wrote their *Tales from Shakespeare* for him when he had moved the business to Holborn. The former **Westminster Jews Free Schools** (rebuilt 1882) can be found quietly decaying away in Hanway Place.

Percy Street was built in the 1760s. The moving spirit here, as elsewhere on the Goodge estate, was a builder called William Franks. The surviving decorative scheme at number 29, the only house still in domestic use, shows a mixture of neo-Classical and late Palladian/Rococo elements, as might be expected, given the date. The White Tower Restaurant was, until 1943, the **Eiffel Tower** and home to one of the few halfway-genuine manifestations of café society in London, after the First War, when the likes of Augustus John, Ronald Firbank and Nancy Cunard made it their own.

In the eighteenth century, the windmill that pumped water to Soho Square (p. 86) used to stand at the west end of Percy Street and one paid a halfpenny to the miller to walk in his grounds. In the later 1920s Augustus John and Nina Hamnett led an exodus from the Eiffel Tower to the **Fitzroy Tavern** round the corner in Charlotte Street. It was this pub that lent its name to the neighbourhood, its literary and artistic denizens and their hangers-on, though they also patronized other locals like the Marquis of Granby and the **Wheatsheaf** at the top of **Rathbone Place**. Indeed by the 1940s the latter was perhaps the most likely place to encounter the poets Dylan Thomas and George Barker; that duet of sodden Scottish painters Robert Colquhoun and Robert

MacBryde; or the neo-Romantics John Minton and Keith Vaughan. The master of ceremonies there was the literary poseur Julian Maclaren-Ross, original of Anthony Powell's character X. Trapnel in his *A Dance to the Music of Time* sequence of novels. By the 1950s radio and television were pulling the intelligentsia westwards to the George and to the Cock in Great Portland Street, handy for the stream of patronage pouring out of nearby Broadcasting House.

All, however, was not lost because **Bertorelli's Restaurant** at this end of **Charlotte Street** became the venue for the Wednesday Club, founded by the art historian Ben Nicolson and Philip Toynbee, then chief reviewer for the *Observer*. Leading lights included the philosopher A. J. Ayer, the historian Hugh Thomas, the poet Stephen Spender, journalists Robert Kee, Maurice Richardson and Peregrine Worsthorne. Beyond Bertorelli's there used to be Schmidt's German Restaurant, serving such delights as *koenigsberger klopfs*, very cheap but with London's rudest waiters. It may have gone, but there are plenty of other restaurants here, and art galleries (Windmill Street has some of these too). Turn right out of Charlotte Street into the pedestrian **Colville Place**, which dates from 1766 and is an extraordinary piece of domesticity to survive so close to the Tottenham Court Road. There are old shop windows, tubs of flowers and a green patch at the end with a wisteria-covered pergola and a few trees. George Gissing, one of the more depressing figures in English literature, lived here at one time. Turn left into **Whitfield Street** and, if you want to visit **Pollock's Toy Museum** or surf the internet at the **Cyberia Café**, cross over Goodge street to **Scala Street**, the next one on, named after the theatre that used to be at its western end.

Benjamin Pollock was the last supplier of Victorian toy theatre sheets, originally a penny for the plain ones and twopence for those that had been hand-coloured. Children cut out the performers and scenery printed on these sheets after pasting them onto cardboard. They could then be used for performing 'Juvenile Drama,' as made clear by the exhibits in room 6 of the Museum. Pollock died in 1937 and his Hoxton shop was then blitzed, but business continued in Monmouth Street, Seven Dials, where the museum began in 1956, before transferring here in 1969. The

The back of an office block in Wells Mews:
in fine weather, sunglasses are a must

Pollock's Toy Museum

small rooms, narrow, winding staircases, red-painted woodwork, low ceilings and creaky floorboards are ideal for the purpose. Here are no flashing lights, buttons to press or electronic bleeps, though *L'Attaque* is displayed next to *War in the Falklands*, among the board games and blow football. There are optical, mechanical and constructional toys (Bayko and Minibrix), tin toys, lead soldiers, puppets including Muffin the Mule, golliwogs, teddy bears and masses of dolls and dolls' houses.

Back to Goodge Street and turn right along it, pausing as you cross Charlotte Street to recall **John Constable**, who lived and painted at number 76 from 1823 until his death in 1837. He was keen to move there with his growing family from Keppel Street where 'we wanted room and were like "bottled wasps on a south wall" '. But there were problems about noxious smells in the studio, until it was found there was a hollow wall connecting its floor directly with the well of the privy below: 'This would have played the devil with the oxygen of my colours.' In the summer months Constable would retreat to Hampstead where he would do 'a good deal of skying', painting cloud studies in support of his belief that the sky is the 'keynote, the standard of scale and the chief organ of sentiment' in landscape. Pioneer though he was, Constable acknowledged his debt to such old masters as Poussin and Claude and their British follower Richard Wilson, who had lived in Charlotte Street fifty years before.

Goodge Place goes off to the right shortly after Charlotte Street, still paved with granite sets, though the pedimented door frames to the late eighteenth-century houses must be recent restorations. Next on the right, stick a nose into **Cleveland Street** to look at the terracotta sunflowers above the ground-floor windows of Cleveland Residences, before heading for **Middlesex Hospital Chapel**, well signposted from the main hall. This is another highly decorated little jewel casket like that at Great Ormond Street (p. 27), designed by J. L. Pearson (Truro Cathedral, St Augustine's Kilburn) and his son (p. 105). Mosaic vies with seventeen different kinds of marble to cover every surface. If you are partial to palindromes do not miss the Greek one on top of the verde antique font, which translates, 'wash away my sin and not only my face'. Its original is in St Sophia in Istanbul. On returning to the hall look at the group of wall paintings by Frederick Cayley Robinson illustrating Acts of Mercy (1915–20). Two show orphans, two doctors; one of the latter includes a group of First World War convalescent soldiers in their blue uniforms.

Berners Street runs south from the hospital and is not worth going down except perhaps for the keystones at ground-floor level on the Berners Hotel, including a lady with plaits and a river god with fish in his hair. It must be recalled, however, that Dickens associated 'The White Woman' with this street.

Dressed entirely in white with a ghastly white plaiting round her head and face inside her white bonnet . . . She is a conceited old creature, cold and formal in manner, and evidently went simpering mad on personal grounds alone – no doubt because a wealthy Quaker wouldn't marry her. This is her bridal dress. She is always walking up here . . . we observe in her mincing step and fishy eye that she intends to lead him a sharp life.

This description, from 'Where We Stopped Growing' in *Miscellaneous Papers*, must be the source of Miss Havisham in *Great Expectations*. Go westwards along **Mortimer Street** from the hospital, past numbers 27 to 35, St Andrew's House, bow-windowed with stone foliage below and pillars between.

Turn left down **Wells Street** and then right into **Margaret Street** and its church of **ALL SAINTS**. This is a building to which it is hard to remain indifferent. Speaking for the antis, David Piper called it 'a formidable and ruthless soul-bashing statement in harsh red brick [with] relentless decoration', in his *Companion Guide to London*. For others it encapsulates the High Anglican 'beauty of holiness'. **William Butterfield** was its architect (1849), he who said his mission was 'to give dignity to brick' but, being a man of his time, felt compelled to build in the Gothic style. Since bricks cannot be carved, he used bands of them in differing colours – black and yellow – to secure decorative effects against the body of red. It is legitimate to see some aggression behind it because it was erected as part of the Tractarian Movement, that counter-attack by parts of the Church of England against a number of threats – Roman Catholic emancipation, and interference by the State from without; unhistorical Bible-bashing evangelicalism within. Since the evangelicals stressed preaching and the

Word, the Tractarians were at pains to emphasise ritual and the sacraments, hence the importance of the chancel and its altar, and then the font, within All Saints. Decorative richness was a legitimate way of glorifying God, and attracting the impoverished inhabitants of this part of London.

The cost of construction was met by **Alexander Beresford-Hope**, a very wealthy Tractarian and Tory M. P. He was the son of Thomas Hope, who had been one of the moving spirits of the Greek Revival fifty years before, and the stepson of one of Wellington's generals, Lord Beresford. His wife was the sister of Lord Salisbury, Prime Minister at the end of the century. As with St George's Bloomsbury, the site was a constricted one, especially since Butterfield had to fit a clergy house and a choir school onto it as well as the church. The style is middle-pointed, regarded as perfection by the Victorian Goths, though to find a precedent for the fancy brickwork one has to look to North Italy or the Tudor period. The nave arches have shafts of polished Peterhead granite topped by Derbyshire alabaster capitals. The poet Gerard Manley Hopkins spoke of the 'touching and passionate curves' of their 'lilyings'. Everywhere are geometrical arrangements of marbles and tiles, with Biblical scenes made up of painted tiles on the walls. The paintings of saints in the vast reredos behind the altar are by Ninian Comper (1909). Whatever the subservience of the Word to the Sacraments, the pulpit is a wonderful confection of different types of marble.

Back into Wells Street, noticing other Victorian-Gothic buildings associated with All Saints as you go, such as number 84 Margaret Street, now the London Fo Kuang Temple. Go into **Wells Mews** opposite the end of Margaret Street for a sight of the startling white-tiled back of an office block by Sir Albert Richardson there. The **Champion** pub on the corner of Wells and Eastcastle Streets has a finely curled iron lantern support and, inside, a series of stained glass portraits of champions: Captain Webb who first swam the Channel, Fred Archer the jockey, Tom Morris who won the Open Golf Championship four times, Florence Nightingale, David Livingstone, W. G. Grace, etc.

Along **Eastcastle Street** past the curious **Welsh Baptist Chapel** (1889) with delicate Corinthian columns and rococo door surround, to the site of the old **Oxford Market** built in 1721 by James Gibbs for the inhabitants of the smart houses further west in Cavendish Square. (Their spiritual needs were looked after by his St Peter's, Vere Street on the further side of the square.) J. T. Smith, sometime pupil of the sculptor Joseph Nollekens and later Keeper of Prints at the British Museum, recalled the miserly Mrs Nollekens shopping there in the 1770s.

When she went to Oxford Market to beat the rounds, in order to discover the cheapest chops, she would walk round several times to give her dog Cerberus an opportunity of picking up scraps. However, of this mode of manoeuvring she was at last ashamed, by the rude remarks of the vulgar butchers . . . 'Here comes Mrs Nollekens and her bull-bitch!'

Continue down Winsley Street to **Oxford Street**. Number 158, **Mappin House**, on the left, was built for the jewellers Mappin and Webb in 1906 by John Belcher and J. J. Joass, among the first architects to take advantage of the freedom allowed by new steel-frame methods of construction to display all kinds of neo-mannerisms in the stone and glass cladding. Turn right, past numbers 164–182, the former **Waring and Gillows** furniture store, in tumescent Edwardian Baroque by R. Frank Atkinson (1901). Such details as its bulls-eye windows are derived from Wren's work at Hampton Court. Note too the corners like ships' prows. Go north again up **Great Titchfield Street** to its junction with Mortimer Street where number 44 is on the site of the Nollekens' home. Joseph Nollekens was as mean as his wife:

The kitchen windows were glazed with glass of a smoky greenish hue, having all the cracked panes carefully puttied. The shelves contained only a bare change of dishes and plates, knives and forks just enough, and those odd ones, the handles of which had undergone a 'sea-change', from a gay pea-green tint, to the yellow tone visible in an overgrown cucumber . . . nor was the sink often stopped with tea-leaves, since they were carefully saved to sprinkle the best carpet, to lay the dust, before it was swept . . . In a small back room Mrs Nollekens had deposited eleven hundred guineas. They were accumulated after the one and two pound notes were issued; for Mrs Nollekens, not trusting in the safety of paper currency, prevailed upon most of her tenants to pay her in gold.

Number 44 Mortimer Street, **Ames House**, began (1904) as a

Edwardian Baroque on Oxford Street, numbers 164–182

All Souls, Langham Place, and Broadcasting House

YWCA hostel; its architect was Beresford Pite, an assistant of John Belcher (p. 71) and in 1901 head of the newly established school of architecture at the Royal College of Art. He was his own man, but with an Arts and Crafts bent, though there is no sculpture here, only tall blank arches and unobtrusive play with different coloured bricks. **Balfour House**, numbers 46 to 54, a very little higher on the right side of Great Titchfield Street, is another hostel by Pite, this time with a bit of sculpture – angels above the doorway. While pausing at this street junction, look a little to the north-east along Mortimer Street to numbers 36 to 38, **Radiant House** (1915), with its turquoise tiles reminiscent of the work of Halsey Ricardo, and open loggia at the top.

Now go westwards along Mortimer Street before doubling back south (left) down Great Portland Street, then sticking your nose left again into **Little Portland Street** for **number 21**. This tall, narrow commercial frontage is Pite at his best, full of subtlety in his treatment of window arches, and culminating in a Diocletian window at the top; yellow brick with plum-coloured horizontal banding. Back into Great Portland Street so as to reach the western end of **Margaret Street** on the right. There is another big Diocletian window on the first floor of **numbers 52 to 53**, above the polished Purbeck marble pillars and columns of the ground floor, and with Gibbs-surround windows at second and third floor levels. This is typical of the many thoroughly enjoyable bits of pre-First War commercial architecture in what is an unfashionable neck of London, though perhaps this is the wrong adjective, given that it also the home of the rag trade. Dillons Bookshop (ex Mowbrays) at **number 28** is another, still better, example by Belcher and Joass, in their telltale mannerist style.

Northwards once more up what is still Regent Street and then right into **Mortimer Street** for a last time, to see Pite giving full rein to his penchant for sculpture at **number 82**. Two Michelangelesque figures are seated on a segmental pediment, their arms raised over their heads as though expecting the aedicule above to collapse at any moment. Spare a glance for **number 93** a little further along on the south side, by Sir John Burnet (p. 46). It is no bigger than many of its neighbours, but uses the grandest classical vocabulary without any bathos.

John Nash's triumphal way from his patrons, the Prince Regent's, long-gone Carlton House up to Regent's Park goes through a chicane, as Regent Street turns into Langham Place at this point. The round portico of Nash's **All Souls** (1822–1824) eases the eye past this local difficulty, the church serving not merely as an eye-catcher at the end of Regent Street, but as a transitional device of the greatest suavity. Its portico columns echoed by those round the spire, All Souls holds its own even though pressed in on by the elephantine bulk of the Langham Hotel across the road and Broadcasting House beyond. Numbers 1 and 3 Riding House Street (1914), attached to the east end of All Souls, are worth a look for the bas reliefs at third-floor level, of almost-nude men and draped women, only some of whom are bare breasted. Maybe gestures towards modesty were made because of proximity to the church.

In some sort of homage to All Souls, maybe, **Broadcasting House** is rounded as well, and inspires in many an affection beyond its aesthetic due, because of the powerful nostalgia for the old BBC. If in doubt about what this means, look at the inscription in the entrance hall beginning *Templum hoc artium et musarum*. The sculptures on Broadcasting House are by **Eric Gill**, who managed to combine fervent Roman Catholicism with a rampant and often deviant sexual life. He chose Prospero and Ariel from Shakespeare's *Tempest* as symbols of broadcasting, but was himself unsure as to why. The main sculpture shows the two of them, while the subsidiary panels are of: Ariel carried up by angels; accompanied by Gaiety and Wisdom; and piping to a group of children. In the hall there is the Sower or Broadcaster. The commission was his most successful piece of public art and made him a celebrity. In part this was brought on by his studied eccentricities. He wouldn't himself listen to the radio, and worked on the carving in the open, whatever the weather, wearing a smock and knee socks. He did not mind the rumour that he wore no underpants and in fact encouraged it by shouting to a friend from the scaffold, 'It's all balls, you know'. When the work was complete the BBC Governors demanded that Ariel's pudenda be reduced in size.

Go eastwards again along **Langham Street** between Broad-

*Numbers 1–2,
Riding House Street*

*Prospero and Ariel, by
Eric Gill, above the doors
of Broadcasting House*

casting House and All Souls. Just before it reaches Great Titchfield Street is the old **Howard de Walden Nurses' Home**, now
the Langham Court Hotel, covered in shiny cream tiles, except
where these are relieved by black chequered ones. Poor nurses, as
if they didn't have to live with such things in their places of work.
Pevsner called it 'a neo-Gothic hygienic aberration' and one can
drink to that in the Crown and Sceptre pub opposite, which has a
padlocked subterranean gents' lavatory outside it, the steps surrounded by elaborate iron railings which are topped by a (more
recent?) openwork lid in the same material. A little way south
down Great Titchfield Street from this point can be seen the **Efes
Restaurant's** ground-floor caryatids in the form of the many-
breasted Goddess Diana of the Ephesians. On eastwards along
Foley Street where, at number 37, the expatriate Swiss painter
Henry Fuseli lived (1741–1825). He was one of the earliest of the
Romantics, as well as a worshipper of Michelangelo, and filled his
work with ghosts, giants, witches and dreaming women, all
imbued with a Mannerist exaggeration of gesture. Indeed, the Sur-
realists might also claim him for their own, with his probings of
the 'two great irrationals', fear and sex, that pervade our dreams.
Judging by his erotic drawings, Fuseli's particular fetish had to do
with elaborate coiffures and elongated necks. He was magnanimous enough to praise Constable's landscapes but claimed that
'he makes me call for my umbrella and greatcoat'. On another
occasion he said, 'Nature puts me out'. His fellow-painter Benjamin Robert Haydon said Fuseli's 'women are all strumpets and
his men all banditti, with the action of galvanised frogs', but
William Blake (p. 111) wrote

> The only Man that e'er I knew
> Who did not make me nearly spew
> Was Fuseli: he was both Turk and Jew –
> And so, dear Christian Friends, how do ye do?

Right into **Candover Street** where York House and Tower House
and the premises of 'T. J. Boulting & Sons, Sanitary and Hot Water
Engineers', running round the corner into **Riding House Street**,
must all be by H. Fuller Clarke (1903). His use of gold against

The old Howard de Walden Nurses' Home, Langham Street

Ironwork surrounding the gents in Foley Street

green mosaic for the lettering recalls the interior decoration of his famous Black Friar pub in Queen Victoria Street in the City. There is another good-looking block of flats, Belmont House, on the east side of Candover Street, perhaps by him too.

Go east along Riding House Street to view one side of Beresford Pite's **All Souls School**, before passing under Middlesex Hospital's bridge of sighs and nipping into Foley Street to see the other side. Several ingredients already noted in his other buildings are here once more (p. 73). The **King and Queen** pub on the corner opposite, with a good lantern bracket, is a rarity, designed in the Gothic style. Continue north up **Cleveland Street** which has little to commend it or detain you, except the memory that in 1889 there was a male brothel at number 19, largely staffed by Post Office telegraph boys. It was patronized by Lord Arthur Somerset, third son of the Duke of Beaufort and Equerry to the Prince of Wales. After it was raided the level of interest, if not downright interference, displayed in the subsequent court cases by powerful figures, lent credence to the rumour that the prince's eldest son, Eddy, Duke of Clarence had also been in the habit of going there.

From telegraph boys to the Telecom Tower seems a natural progression, though we must now call it the **BT TOWER**, and it began life as the Post Office Tower. The rationale behind it is something called microwave radio, on whose invisible beams TV programmes, telephone conversations and computer data can be transmitted, but only as far as the eye can see. Hills and tall buildings interrupt them, hence the need for the Tower to be 189 metres high, so the beams from its horn and dish-shaped aerials can reach the first of the microwave towers round London. These then feed the rest of the countrywide network of towers. Before this system was established the only way to send television programmes was by cable links and local transmitters.

Work on the Tower began in 1961 and it was completed in 1965, at a cost of £2.5 million. It was a popular tourist attraction, with hundreds of thousands whizzing up each year in the high-speed lifts that take only thirty seconds to get to the top. It also had the inevitable revolving restaurant up there. But all these came to a stop in October 1971 when a bomb exploded on the thirty-first floor. No-one claimed responsibility for it and no-one was injured, but it deprived millions of a simple pleasure because the Tower has been closed to the public since, though the restaurant stayed open until 1980.

Turn right into Maple Street at the Tower's foot and then left into **Conway Street**. Number 1 on the left is the glass-fronted office of the architect Nicholas Grimshaw, he of the Eurotunnel terminal at Waterloo and other interesting buildings in Docklands. Offcuts from various systems of jointing, ribbing, etc, are displayed in the window, like so many pieces of sculpture. **FITZROY SQUARE** now opens up before you. This is part of what was called, confusingly, the Southampton Estate, which belonged to the Fitzroy family, Earls of Euston and Dukes of Grafton. The other main element of the estate was Euston Square, to the east, which has vanished now. The south and east sides of Fitzroy Square were built in the 1790s to the designs of **Robert Adam**. The south side received much bomb damage in the Blitz, but that has been made good, so it can be enjoyed again, with the divided premises of the London Foot Hospital at either end – one for left feet, the other for right? Indeed the whole square is now a source of quiet but intense pleasure, even though the north and west sides were not completed until 1828 and lack the urbane distinction of Adam's neo-Classical elevations. Traffic is excluded from it, and its circular garden is well kept, with new railings and ivy carefully trained up the trunks of the plane trees. But the pebble-dash litter bins and ugly benches could be improved on.

The Pre-Raphaelite painter **Ford Madox Brown** (*The Last of England, Work*) moved to number 37 in 1865 from Highgate after a successful one-man retrospective, about the first of its kind. For some eight years he and his wife Emma held their famous fortnightly evenings here to entertain fellow Pre-Raphaelites, political refugees, distinguished foreigners such as Turgenev, Mark Twain, Liszt, and Cosima Wagner; and Tennyson, Browning and Swinburne. Ford and Emma sang duets round the piano decorated by William Morris and much poetry was recited. There was a rift in the domestic bliss when Ford fell in love with Marie Spartali, one of the 'Stunners' often painted by Dante Gabriel Rossetti. It was the marriage of the Browns' daughter to William Michael Rossetti, Christina and Dante's brother, which caused

Fitzroy Square

A former dairy in Warren Street

Christina's move to Torrington Square in 1874 (p. 52).

In 1907 the square became an outpost for the Bloomsbury Group when **Virginia Woolf** moved to number 29 with her brother Adrian Stephen. The marriage of their sister Vanessa to Clive Bell had broken up the Gordon Square household (p. 54). **George Bernard Shaw** had been living at the same Fitzroy Square address from 1887 until 1898. Duncan Grant and J. M. Keynes were at number 22 at the same time as Virginia Woolf was at number 29. In 1911 they all decamped to the north side of Brunswick Square (p. 21). But Bloomsbury connections did not end then because in 1913 the critic and painter **Roger Fry** set up the **Omega Workshop** at number 33. He employed fellow artists to decorate and finish furnishings designed mostly by himself and Vanessa Bell, but only for three and a half days a week, so they also had time for their own work. It was production-line stuff but no doubt many were glad of the regular money it brought in.

A little earlier the painter Walter Sickert took a studio, which had once been Whistler's, at number 8 **Fitzroy Street**. This runs north and south from the east side of the square. A group of artists – including William and Albert Rothenstein, Spencer Gore, Walter Russell, Harold Gilman and Charles Ginner – soon co-alesced round him, and decided to take two rooms at number 19. Here they held open house every Saturday afternoon, acting as their own dealers and selling their scenes of ordinary domestic life. In 1911 they realigned themselves into the Camden Town Group. These houses have all disappeared but there is one curiosity to see in the street, just round from the south-east corner of the square: the statue of General Francisco de Miranda (1750–1815). He was the 'precursor of Latin American independence', born in Venezuela, dying a prisoner in Spain. He is here because for some years he lived at number 58 Grafton Way, where Simon Bolivar came to meet him in 1810.

Leave the square by its north-west corner and on the corner of Conway Street and **Warren Street**, the cream and blue tiles of **J. Evans, Dairy Farmer**'s shop make a nice splash. Warren Street used to seethe with second-hand motor traders wheeling and dealing up and down, but it is quiet and refurbished now. You can go home from Great Portland Street or Warren Street tubes.

WALK FOUR

From Soho Square to Chinatown

Set out from Tottenham Court Road tube southwards down Charing Cross Road and take the first right, Sutton Row, which will bring you into Soho Square, the obvious starting point for **SOHO**. The name seems to have been derived from a hunting call, So Ho! – along the lines of Yoicks, Tally Ho. The identity of the developers who put paid to the hunting fields in the later seventeenth century is preserved in the street names: Frith, Compton, Pulteney, Wardour. Soho Square began by being highly fashionable, helped by Charles II's bastard, the Duke of Monmouth, having a house on its south side. His followers even used 'Soho!' as their rallying cry in his rebellion against his uncle, James II. Other more modest streets soon attracted the first of many succeeding waves of emigrants: the Protestant Huguenots expelled from Catholic France, who established a tradition of excellence in the decorative and applied arts in the area.

By the 1750s, according to the novelist Henry Fielding, 'the people of fashion retreated before the foe to Hanover Square; whence they were once more driven to Grosvenor Square and even beyond it'. By the end of the century many houses had been subdivided for multi-occupancy and the population went steeply up as the poor piled in. In the later nineteenth century, rents went up because of pressure from the vice trade, and the respectable workers were priced out. The vicar of St Anne's Soho mounted the first of many 'clean up Soho' campaigns. In the 1880s Shaftesbury Avenue had been created as a means of getting rid of the worst slums of South Soho. As the Jews began to pour in from Eastern Europe many found their way here, and Italians likewise. The former did tailoring work for Savile Row on the respectable further side of Regent Street, while the latter worked in the restaurants which were starting to be a part of West End life.

Outside the Camisa delicatessen, Old Compton Street

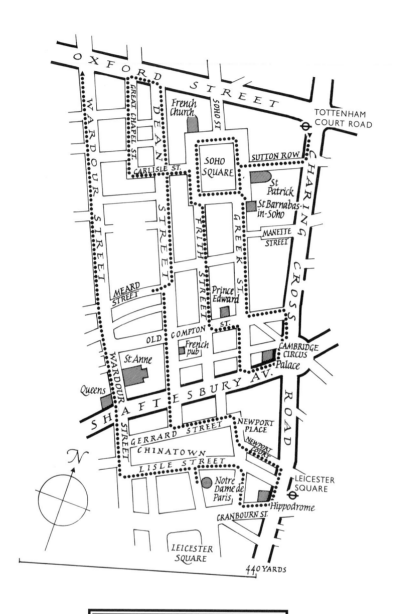

WALK FOUR

Between the wars the habit of eating out really got a grip and Soho was happy to cater for the taste. After dinner, the smart set went on to the Hon. David Tennant's Gargoyle Club in Meard Street or Ma Meyrick's '43' Club in Gerrard Street. The Messina brothers dominated the brothels in the 1930s and 40s, but as time went on dirty book and magazine shops, strip clubs and clip joints, all 'protected' by corrupt police, became the name of the game. The 1959 Obscene Publications Act and Street Offences Act, instead of curbing this, gave it a great boost, aided by the fact that the heads of the Obscene Publications Squad and the Serious Crime Branch of the Metropolitan Police were both bent, and not arrested until 1976. The clean-up then removed the big boys but allowed small fry to come in with peep shows and massage parlours. The spiral of squalor was only stopped once locals started organising themselves and pressuring Westminster Council. New licensing laws for sex shops and places of entertainment finally brought things under control in the 1980s, by which time rising rents in rejuvenated Covent Garden were making Soho a very attractive office location for bustling young design, media, advertising and film businesses. New 'designer' restaurants, wine bars and cafés sprang up to cater for them, turning the area into a magnet for foodies. In 1995 Terence Conran opened the Mezzo Restaurant in Wardour Street, one of the biggest in Europe, seating 700.

For the locals, the sleaze has gone, except round the junction of Brewer with Rupert Street, but the new invasion means their sons and daughters can no longer afford to live in the area and the small businesses and craft workshops are put under great pressure. Some would say that Soho has become a theme park: too fashionable and too self-conscious for its own good. It has been cleaned up, but a lot of the flavour that attracted the artists and writers in the grey post-war years has gone. As a *Sunday Times* headline put it in an article on Soho in 1987, 'Goodbye sex, hello style.' One could not describe it now as George Melly remembers it in the 1950s: 'that dodgy never-never land, that hallucinated enclave, where we waited, consumed by angst, to cure today's hangover by making certain of tomorrow's.'

Soho Square was developed by Richard Frith, a big builder and property man who, like so many of his type, died insolvent after a spell in a debtors' prison. The rascally Nicholas Barbon (p. 26), who was mainly active further south in Gerrard Street and with the Newport estate, tried to get a slice of the action by buying leases at strategic points, but was presumably bought off. One's eye is first caught by the peculiar half-timbered Wendy-house in the middle of the Square's garden, which only dates from 1876 and is used by the gardeners. The statue of Charles II by Caius Cibber next to it originally had statues of English rivers at its base. The sculptor Joseph Nollekens as a boy lived in Dean Street nearby:

> I have often stood for hours together, to see the water run out of the jugs of the old river-gods into the basin in the middle of the square, but the water never would run except when the windmill was going round at the top of Rathbone Place.

The windmill pumped water from a spring there (p. 65). In the 1870s the statues were removed to a house called Grims Dyke near Harrow, which later became the home of W. S. Gilbert. It was his widow who bequeathed Charles II back to the square.

The square starts its numbering, clockwise, towards its north-west corner where number 2 is occupied by Bloomsbury Books, the publishers. They act as a reminder that A & C Black were in this corner for many years, and that George Routledge was at number 36 from 1843 to 1858, where Rupert Hart-Davis, one of the most distinguished publishers of the post-war years, followed him 100 years later. Number 3, home of the British Board of Film Classification, by a nice irony was occupied by Richard Payne Knight from 1809: as well as assembling an outstanding collection of classical antiquities and 250 drawings by Claude, which he left to the British Museum, he was notorious as the author of an illustrated book on phallic worship, *An Account of the Remains of the Worship of Priapus*. The house has been rebuilt and now has an interesting Arts and Crafts frontage incorporating convex and concave curves and some lively plaster trees in relief (1903). In 1816 the Soho Bazaar was set up at numbers 4 to 6 by John Trotter, who had done well from his involvement in government stores in the Napoleonic Wars. Its purpose, he claimed, was 'the encouragement of Female and Domestic Industry' and to stop the country pouring its 'happy and innocent virgins into the common sink of London'. Instead they were to sell their handiwork from stalls in the bazaar which they hired by the day. The millinery, gloves, lace, jewellery, etc., sold well and it continued until 1889 when A. & C. Black moved in.

The French Protestant Church (1893), by Aston Webb, is on the north side. It does not look much like a church, but then its sombre terracotta and brick, and the steep green slate roof topped by a black Arts and Crafts lantern, seem well suited to the denomination of its worshippers. It is an unexpected effort from an architect one associates much more with buildings like the Admiralty Arch. A naively carved tympanum (1950) shows Edward VI giving sanctuary to early Huguenots in 1550. Numbers 10 and 15 are both late seventeenth-century, while the north-east corner was occupied by a notorious brothel called Hooper's Hotel, until it became the headquarters of Crosse & Blackwell. They had a jam and bottling factory in Fauconberg Mews behind, a particularly louring cul-de-sac, and only moved out in 1920.

In 1760 a continental adventuress called **Mrs Theresa Cornelys** arrived in London. She had been born in Venice in 1723, the daughter of an Austrian actor, and among her lovers had been the Margrave of Bayreuth and Prince Charles of Lorraine. By 1753 she was back in Venice, where she had a daughter by Casanova. Her attempt to launch herself as a singer in London was a flop, but the subscription evenings she then began at Carlisle House, where St Patrick's Roman Catholic church now is, were a success from the start. Like any astute night club owner today, she made them attractive by appearing to limit access to them: entrance was by prepaid ticket only. At first they offered music and card playing but soon she was organising masquerades and balls. Concert and banqueting rooms were built down Sutton Row and the premises were redecorated at regular intervals. In 1771 she started staging operas there, avoiding the King's Theatre, Haymarket's monopoly by calling them Harmonic Meetings. As Horace Walpole cattily recounted,

She had the assurance to advertise that the subscription was to provide coals for the poor, for she has vehemently courted the mob, and succeeded in gaining their princely favour. She then declared her masquerades were for the benefit of commerce. I concluded she would open a bawdy house next for the interest of the Foundling Hospital and I am not quite mistaken, for they say one of her maids . . . affirms that she could not undergo the fatigue of making the beds so often.

Unfortunately Mrs Cornely's business acumen did not match her invention and her goods were often seized because of non-payment of debts. But the biggest blow was the opening of the Pantheon in 1772, where Marks and Spencer now, is to the north of Great Marlborough Street. It was a huge, elegantly decorated rotunda especially designed by James Wyatt for public entertainment. Mrs Cornelys struggled on intermittently at Carlisle House until 1778, and even after her departure 'promenades', as they were now called, continued there. William Hickey remembered that in 1780,

Mrs Cornelys's truly magnificent suite of apartments upon the principal floor were opened every Sunday night at seven o'clock, for the reception of company. So much did it take that the first people of the kingdom attended it, as did also the whole beauty of the metropolis, from the Duchess of Devonshire down to the little milliner's apprentice from Cranbourn Alley. The crowd from eight to twelve was immense.

However, fickle fashion must have moved on again because, after anti-Catholic regulations were eased in 1791, the ballroom at Carlisle House was bought the following year and converted into a church. The rest had already been demolished. The first priest there was Father O'Leary and you will see the modest neo-classical memorial to him (1802) as you enter the present Italianate red brick **St Patrick's Church**, with its campanile, built in 1893. Its interior is uncannily reminiscent of some dim church in a provincial Italian town. Above the holy water stoup in the porch there is a decent Baroque marble statue of the dead Christ in the arms of his mother, which has been covered in crude gold paint, except where the touch of the faithful has worn it away from Christ's foot.

Number 22 was where Alderman William Beckford lived from 1751 to 1770. He was a man of great wealth, derived from West Indian sugar, but best remembered as the father of William Beckford, the author of *Vathek* and builder of that colossal Gothick

*Soho Square: the Wendy house
and Charles II*

*Manhattan in
Old Compton Street*

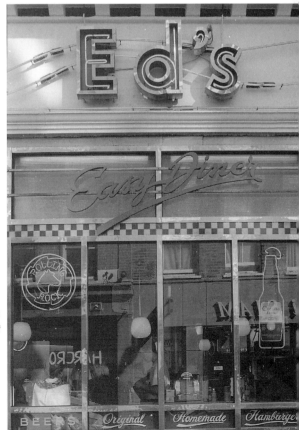

folly, Fonthill. Number 26, with its large first-floor Venetian window, was built, along with number 25 (demolished), by Sir William Robinson of Newby Hall in North Yorkshire. Number 26 was furnished by Thomas Chippendale for £469. Next to it is number 1, Greek Street, the premises of a charity called **The House of St Barnabas-in-Soho**. It was built, as a shell only, in 1746, but in 1754 Richard Beckford, brother of William, took it and had it decorated with some of the best quality Rococo plaster-work in London, although its door frames and friezes are Palladian. Like his brother, Richard was both an Alderman of the City of London and an MP. He did not long enjoy his house because he died at Lyons in 1756.

The plasterwork is well worth seeing (ring 0171 437 1894), particularly that on the staircase and in the Council Room on the first floor. The central ceiling relief has the Four Elements – Earth, Air, Fire, Water – portrayed by fat putti, while the Four Seasons are in the corners. The dragons on the east wall are said to refer to the coat-of-arms of the City of London, rather than just a touch of Chinoiserie. The chimneypiece and overmantel are modern replacements because three of the originals were sold – for £350 – in 1864 to help pay for the chapel.

In 1810 the house was let to the Westminster and Middlesex Sewer Board and later was used by the Metropolitan Board of Works after it was founded in 1855, but in 1862 the House of Charity, as it was then known, moved in. This body had been founded round the corner in Manette Street in 1846 by Gladstone, F. D. Maurice (p. 26) and a number of other high-minded lay Anglicans, to offer immediate succour to the homeless poor. No inmate was allowed to remain longer than a month and daily church attendance was expected, hence the tiny chapel, which can also be visited, with its patch of garden and big plane tree by it. It is very correct architecturally, thirteenth-century Gothic, richly decorated with mosaic and marble but given a quaintness by its compression. Go round into Manette Street to see its gold and red banded sandstone exterior, and also the former workhouse (1770) by James Paine Jr next to it, where the charity began. Manette Street was Rose Street until renamed in the nineteenth century after the doctor in Dickens' *A Tale of Two Cities*, whose lodgings were supposed to be at number 1, Greek Street. This now offers a refuge only to women referred to it by the social services or other charities, so they can find their feet before moving on to somewhere more permanent. As you leave it, notice the massive chain on the front door and the two stone obelisks outside it, which would originally have supported iron lamps and conical snuffers.

Continuing round Soho Square, Allsops the estate agents occupy the site of the building at the top of Greek Street where **Thomas de Quincey** took refuge in 1803, having fled to London from Manchester to escape his guardians, as he described in *Confessions of an English Opium Eater*. It belonged to Mr Brunell, the attorney who worked in harness with the money-lender whom de Quincey had approached. Brunell denied himself 'all indulgence in the luxury of too delicate a conscience'.

Towards nightfall I went down to Greek Street; and found, on taking possession of my new quarters, that the house already contained one single inmate, a poor, friendless child, apparently ten years old; but she seemed hungerbitten; and sufferings of that sort often make children look older than they are. . . From the want of furniture, the noise of the rats made a prodigious uproar on the staircase and hall; so that, amidst the real fleshly ills of cold and hunger, the forsaken child had found leisure to suffer still more from the self-created one of ghosts. . . We lay upon the floor, with a bundle of law-papers for a pillow, but with no other covering than a large horseman's cloak; afterwards, however, we discovered in a garret an old sofa-cover, a small piece of rug, and some fragments of other articles, which added a little to our comfort. The poor child crept close to me for warmth, and for security against her ghostly enemies. . . Meantime, the master of the house sometimes came in upon us suddenly, and very early; sometimes not till ten o'clock; sometimes not at all. He was in constant fear of arrest.

Then follows the Hospital for Women, largely empty and boarded up. The south-west corner of the square was, from 1777, for many years the London home of Sir Joseph Banks, President of the Royal Society, who accompanied Captain Cook on one of his voyages to the South Seas. His Thursday morning breakfasts for passing savants or aspiring scientists and travellers were famous and he also allowed them the use of his library and collections there. The houses on either side of the exit to Carlisle Street both have bows projecting into it and both have nineteenth-century shop fronts, number 37 using the Doric and number 38 the Corinthian order.

Leave the square by way of **Greek Street**, a constituent of one of London's very few areas laid out on a grid plan. In 1676, John Georgirenes, the former Bishop of Samos, arrived in England, a refugee from one of the Ottoman Empire's periodic crack-downs on the Orthodox Church, and was taken under the protection of the Bishop of London. Perhaps wisely, Georgirenes turned down the offer of a site for a church from Nicholas Barbon (pp. 26 and 86) and took instead one from his fellow-bishop, where St Martin's School of Art now stands in Charing Cross Road. But before the church was completed, squabbles among his expatriate flock broke out, and the building ended up instead as one of five Huguenot chapels in Soho in the 1690s.

Number 2 Greek Street is the Gay Hussar restaurant. It has long been the haunt, if not of champagne, then of tokai and Hungarian goulash socialists. Just how long it has been around is indicated by the adjective in its title. Number 3 is Milroy's the whisky shop, which stocks over 300 varieties. The sign of the bogus half-timbered pub, the Pillars of Hercules, by the entry to Manette Street, is a good one. (Note, next to it, the premises of Swish Publications.) Numbers 17 and 21 have the remains of good early nineteenth-century shop fronts, while number 18's is curiously constructed from stone, and dates from 1863. It housed the Establishment Club, run by Peter Cook with the money he was earning from *Beyond The Fringe*, for a year or two, until the satire bubble burst in 1963. On the right, at number 48, is the Escargot restaurant, another Soho survivor though its decor and style are now fiercely up-to-date. At the junction with Old Compton Street stands the **Prince Edward Theatre**, 1930. Its bruised-plum coloured brickwork, recessed pointing, brass torchères and roof with a pagoda tilt certainly make it distinctive. Its longest recent run was eight years of *Evita*, but it has been used as a cinema more often than not.

Turn left into **Old Compton Street** so that you can look at numbers 1 to 3, on the corner with Charing Cross Road, a splen-

Edwardian Baroque: Old Compton Street

Late Victorian Flemish Renaissance:
The Palace Theatre, Cambridge Circus

did bit of Edwardian Baroque by R. J. Worley who also built 3 Soho Square. It is a combination of green-glazed tiles and crisp, chunky stonework. Some Art Nouveau tilework is just visible above the door and one would love to know if it survives underneath the fascia of Lovejoy's bookshop. (There is in fact a reprise of numbers 1 to 3 at the west end of the same block.)

To the south is **Cambridge Circus** and the enormously enjoyable turreted and curved terracotta frontage of the **Palace Theatre**, built by Thomas Collcutt in 1890 and launched by Richard D'Oyly Carte as the Royal English Opera House, to encourage home-grown productions. But, after Sullivan's *Ivanhoe*, these were not forthcoming, so he sold out to Augustus Harris, the very successful manager of Drury Lane, in 1892. Having done Sardou's *Cleopatra*, Sarah Bernhardt was already in rehearsal for Oscar Wilde's *Salome* in that year when it was banned by the Lord Chamberlain because it contained Biblical characters. Betjeman called the Palace 'more impressive within and without than Covent Garden' and certainly its concave François-Premier or Flemish Renaissance front and marble, alabaster and onyx interior are worthy of the money Andrew Lloyd Webber spent restoring them.

Behind the Palace turn right into Greek Street again. Kettners Restaurant was founded in 1868 by a French chef of that name, though its menu now is dominated by pizzas. On the right, Maison Bertaux pâtisserie is also an institution. Next to it is the Coach and Horses pub, its landlord and its bores made famous by Jeffrey Bernard in his long-running weekly column 'Low Life' in the *Spectator*. Turn left into **Old Compton Street**, going west this time. Wheeler's, the original of that chain of fish restaurants where oysters were first sold in 1929, is at numbers 19 to 21. The painters Francis Bacon and Lucian Freud made it their own in the 1950s; 'Oysters and despair – the diet of my life', according to the former. Its green bricks and pointing picked out in white is challenged by the Soho Brasserie next door, done out in purple and lilac, which a Thai restaurant to the north attempts to trump in pink. Also, to the west, two long-term survivors: the Pâtisserie Valérie and the Algerian Coffee Stores, selling teas and herbal infusions as well. But the coffee bars of the 1950s, like Heaven and Hell and the Two I's, where Tommy Steele was discovered, have long gone. On

Old Compton Street: What the well-dressed chef is wearing, at Denny's; and tea in the Algerian Coffee Stores

Saturday nights these days, the street becomes an informal pedestrian precinct.

Now we head north again up the grid, along **Frith Street**, which has eighteenth- and early nineteenth-century houses at various points throughout its length, with numbers 60 to 64 at the north-west end the oldest (late seventeenth-century). However, the doorcase of number 60 is 1778. Back south, John Logie Baird first demonstrated television upstairs at number 22. Mozart and his family, having moved from Cecil Court to Ebury Street in Chelsea for the summer of 1764, then lodged at number 21 from September until the middle of 1765. Ronnie Scott's Club, the London home of jazz, is opposite. The owner is famous for his repartee, such as threatening to send for 'Igor with his genital clamps', to get the audience to shut up. Number 15, now a Café Rouge, has an excellent early nineteenth-century gothick shop front, and the Swedish bar next door is worth a mention for its nausea-inducing name – Garlic & Shots.

On the left, the Dog and Duck pub at the Bateman Street junction features these animals in tilework, mosaic and bas-relief at various points on walls and floor. At number 49, Alastair Little's restaurant was in the 1980s vanguard, and chefs have gone forth from it to spread the gospel. The elegant Hazlitt's Hotel occupies numbers 6 and 7 (1718) at the top on the right. **William Hazlitt**, the essayist, critic, radical and painter, died at number 6 in September 1830. In 1803 Coleridge called him

a thinking, observant, original man . . . His manners are ninety-nine in a hundred singularly repulsive: brow hanging, shoe contemplative, strange . . . He is, I verily believe, kindly natured . . . He is strongly confused and dark in his conversation and delivers himself of almost all his conceptions with a forceps, yet he says more than any man I ever knew.

In 1804 Coleridge scribbled in his notebook: 'May we all avoid Hazlitts on jury!' By 1829, when he came to rest in Frith Street, he had long regarded Coleridge, Wordsworth and Southey as apostates, betrayers of the cause of Liberty and the People. His second wife had recently left him and he was deeply engaged in a Life of Napoleon, whom he saw as 'the child and champion of the Revolution, the bulwark between . . . the Peoples of Europe and hereditary despotisms'. A myth grew up that he died abandoned and destitute, perhaps because of a note he sent to Francis Jeffrey in 1830: 'Dear Sir, I am dying; can you send me £10 and so consummate your many kindnesses to me?' In fact his son was tending to him, he was not penniless, and Jeffrey was then no longer editor of the *Edinburgh Review*, to which Hazlitt had been contributing. The epitaph on his original tombstone close by in St Anne's churchyard, Wardour Street, said among much else, 'He lived to see his deepest wishes gratified . . . to see the downfall of the Bourbons and some prospect of good to mankind . . . He was the first (unanswered) metaphysician of the age . . . a burning wound to an aristocracy . . . ' (Charles X had been driven from France in July 1830.)

Go up the west side of Soho Square once more and turn left into **Carlisle Street**, which continues across Dean Street. Number 6 houses the offices of *Private Eye*, formerly in Greek Street, and was once the home of Handel's right-hand man, Christopher Smith. Turn right at the end into Great Chapel Street. While walking up it, look left into both Sheraton and Hollen Streets to see the side façades of the old premises of Novellos, the music publishers, the main frontage of which is in Wardour Street (p. 105). That in **Hollen Street** has jolly bas-reliefs of putti having singing lessons at one end and working a printing press at the other. On the north side of the street is 'Henry Heath's Hat Factory', as stone-cut lettering on the front proclaims: a handsome building with metal glazing bars, and red-brick pilasters and window arches standing out from London stock bricks for the main body.

Double back into **Dean Street**, once you reach Oxford Street, and you will be rewarded by more putti on the terracotta bow windows of number 1. Number 6 is a good early nineteenth-century warehouse, in fact the back of the Soho Bazaar (p. 86), while number 8 is Gothic red brick from 1878 – quite late. **Number 88**, on the right, is a lovely delicate rococo shop front from 1791, again quite late for that style. Do not omit to peer through the windows of numbers 13 and 14 opposite for a view of the sculpture collection enlivening the premises of 'Real Creatives Worldwide Ltd'.

Number 78 houses **Allen and Fraser**, Solicitors, established in 1788, but located here from 1833. As a notice proclaims, they act as 'Clerks to the Board of Green Cloth, Verge of the Palace of St

Dean Street: a typical corner pub and the rococo shopfront at number 88, next to it

James's, etc.' The Board is the last surviving court of the royal prerogative, responsible for licensing pubs and gambling within the area of the old royal Palace of Whitehall. This includes the northern end of Whitehall, Carlton House Terrace and the National Gallery. Some of the buildings occupied by the Quo Vadis restaurant, another Soho survivor founded in 1926, go back to the 1690s, but its real claim to fame is that **Karl Marx** inflicted a miserable existence on his family when they lodged in the upstairs rooms for several years, while he researched *Das Kapital* in the Reading Room of the British Museum.

Number 76 is a grand sort of eighteenth-century house and contains some wall paintings of ships from that period. Number 75 was grand too, but in spite of being subject to the first-ever preservation order in 1913, it was dismantled in 1923, with its staircase and ground-floor rooms ending in the Art Institute of Chicago. Until 1938 there used to be a small theatre, the Royalty, where numbers 72 to 74 now are. Its record of West End premières was formidable: *Trial By Jury* 1875, *Ghosts* 1891, *Widowers' Houses* and *Charley's Aunt* 1892, *Wild Duck* 1894, *You Never Can Tell* 1899, *The Vortex* 1924.

Meard Street, off to the right, is one of Soho's proudest possessions now, an almost-complete enclave of eighteenth-century houses still with their railings, their window surrounds in lighter red brick standing out against the near-black brickwork of the walls. Numbers 67 and 68 Dean Street, on its corner, are of the same vintage. On the left of Dean Street, number 44 is the **Groucho Club**, so called after the Marx brother (no relation to him higher up the street) who said he wouldn't want to be a member of any club that didn't throw him out. Founded in the 1980s, it sees itself as at the very epicentre of that self-regarding world of the media and modern publishing. If it symbolises the new Soho, then the **French Pub**, at number 49 (now called the French House, formerly the York Minster), was certainly a representative institution of what went before. Its famous patron, Gaston Berlemont, retired in 1989 after seventy-five years living on the premises, which became the unofficial headquarters of the Free French in the Second World War.

After crossing Shaftesbury Avenue, Dean Street turns briefly into Macclesfield Street where the Dutch had their wartime drinking hole at **De Hems** pub, which still flourishes. The smell, the street signs in English and Chinese characters, and the passers-by will inform you that you are now entering one of London's latest acquisitions: **CHINATOWN**. Limehouse in Docklands had been home to the Chinese, but it was badly bombed in the Blitz. This, the inroads made by the washing machine on their traditional trade, the clearance of many prostitutes out of Soho in the 1960s, and a rush by Hong Kong Chinese to beat a ban on Commonwealth immigrants in 1965, brought about their takeover of Gerrard Street and Lisle Street and the explosion of Chinese restaurants in the area. Now there are Chinese triumphal arches and even the telephone boxes have been given the Chinoiserie look. This neat historical explanation has to be qualified by the fact that there was a Maxim's Chinese Restaurant in Gerrard Street between the wars – the original of Anthony Powell's *Casanova's Chinese Restaurant*.

Nicholas Barbon developed **Gerrard Street** around 1685; in the eighteenth century there used to be a tavern called the Turk's Head at number 9, at present the Loon Moon supermarket. It was here in 1763 that Joshua Reynolds founded The Club, 'in order to give Dr Johnson unlimited opportunities for talking'. Edmund Burke and Oliver Goldsmith were among the original members and when Garrick returned from abroad in 1765 he said to Reynolds, 'I like it much, I think I should be one of you.' On hearing this, Johnson exclaimed, 'He'll be one of us! How does he know we will permit him? The first duke in England has no right to hold such language.' But by 1773 Garrick was a member. Number 40 opposite was the home of the great Huguenot silversmith, Paul de Lamerie. Edmund Burke, James Boswell and John Dryden also lived in Gerrard Street at various times. Number 14 is a Victorian extravaganza of rubbed and moulded yellow brick.

Newport Place at the east end of Gerrard Street doesn't stand much of a chance, with the back of Richard Seifert's Shaftesbury Avenue fire station to one side and a harsh development of flats and shops, built out of repellent smooth-textured red brick, on another. This replaces a tenement block bombed in April 1941 with the loss of forty-eight lives. **Newport Court**, on the other hand, has a row of late seventeenth-century houses dating from Barbon's development of the site of Newport House. This had been the home of Francis Newport, Earl of Bradford, who married a daughter of the Earl of Bedford who developed Covent Garden.

Turn right into Charing Cross Road and almost immediately you will be outside the **Hippodrome**, built by Frank Matcham in 1900 as an arena where the most lavish spectacles could be staged. The central circus area was poised on hydraulic rams, while the lowest level could be filled with 100,000 gallons from the Cran Bourne (stream), which conveniently flows beneath. Divers could plunge in from the dome, which opened to reveal the sky; twenty elephants could slide down a shute into the pool. One show featured seventy polar bears. At the Little Newport Street end, notice two surviving mosaic panels of sprays and crowns in green and gold. The building is still topped by a charioteer and horses on a peculiar ribbed pedestal.

Go north up Leicester Court into **Lisle Street**. Then go left almost immediately into Leicester Place to see the French church, **Notre Dame de Paris**. This owes its circular shape to the fact that its predecessor, destroyed in the Blitz, had, until 1861, been the Leicester Place Rotunda. Various panoramas, such as one of the Battle of Waterloo, were on show in it. One of the side chapels has frescoes by Jean Cocteau and there are eight scenes from the life of the Virgin on the pillars by students from the Beaux Arts de Paris. At the top of Leicester Place the vista is closed by the terrace on the north side of Lisle Street with its date, 1792, in the pediment, built after the demolition of Leicester House. This is solid Chinatown again. A little to the west the Flemish renaissance front of the old **St John's Hospital** for Diseases of the Skin, with its stepped gable, looks unloved, perhaps because the area is now full of Chinese herbal medicine centres to deal with such complaints. It was built in 1897 by Treadwell and Martin (p. 63)

The west end of Lisle Street brings you into **Wardour Street**. Look left at the startling number 3, recently built in bright blue glazed brick, and at number 9 (1798), boldly labelled 'Exchange and Bullion Office'. Then turn right. Number 32 in brown glazed brick has a mannered pediment, then number 41 to 43 is Arts and

Lisle Street, where even the pub signs are in Chinese, and the former St John's Hospital

Crafts, with Art Nouveau trim round the door, and an elegant bracket supporting the clock. It was the premises of Clarkson's Theatrical Wig Shop, whose foundation stone was laid by Sarah Bernhardt in 1904 and its coping stone by Henry Irving in 1905. At the junction with Shaftesbury Avenue, there is the **Queen's Theatre**, built in 1907 by W. G. R. Sprague, and the first where one didn't have to wear evening dress in the dress circle. It was damaged in World War II, hence the nasty 1957 façade, but its interior survives – less obviously Louis XVI neo-classical in feel than some of Sprague's auditoriums, with perhaps a hint of the Baroque. Its domed ceiling incorporates eight seated female figures. (For more on Sprague, Matcham and the other theatre designers of the West End, see the companion volume on Covent Garden and the Strand.)

St Anne's, Soho owes its foundation to an anonymous lady benefactor who gave £5000 to the Bishop of London in 1676 to build a church where it was most needed. There is argument over whether Wren was its architect, unlikely to be settled now that his nave has vanished, destroyed in the Blitz. The present idiosyncratic spire dates from 1801 and was designed by S. P. Cockerell. John Betjeman best summed it up in the verses he wrote when an appeal for a new church was launched in 1976:

> High up in the air two barrels interlock
> To form the faces of this famous clock.
> Reduced to drawing-room size this clock would be
> A Paris ornament of 1803.

His efforts and those of many others bore fruit and a new church, community centre, offices and flats to the east of the tower were completed in 1991. The Soho Society is based here and enquiries can be answered every afternoon. The churchyard is six feet above the level of Wardour Street, thanks to the countless thousands of burials in it over the centuries. The modern tablet to William Hazlitt (p. 96) is below that to **King Theodore of Corsica**. Baron Theodore von Neuhoff was a Westphalian adventurer who, in 1736, after supplying them with stores and arms, persuaded the Corsican patriots to elect him King and then led them against their Genoese overlords. After a few months he left the island to seek assistance, and was never to return, although the English took up his cause in 1743. By then he had no adherents left in Corsica. When he was imprisoned for debt in 1750 Horace Walpole was obviously fascinated by the idea of a king on his uppers, and commissioned Hogarth to make a portrait of him, but it has not survived. Then in 1753 Walpole promoted a subscription for him in a newspaper, when he was again in prison.

His Majesty's character is so bad, that it only raised £50; though that was much above his desert, it was so much below his expectation that he sent a solicitor to threaten the printer with a prosecution for having taken so much liberty with his name – take notice too that he had accepted the money.

When he died in 1756, Walpole arranged for his memorial in St Anne's, and composed the inscription and verses. The former states Theodore died 'immediately after leaving the King's Bench Prison by the benefit of the Act of Insolvency [a new piece of legislation], in consequence of which he registered his kingdom of Corsica for the use of his creditors.'

> The grave, great teacher, to a level brings
> Heroes and beggars, galley slaves and Kings,
> But Theodore this moral learn'd ere dead;
> Fate poured its lessons on his Livinig [*sic*] head,
> Bestow'd a Kingdom, and denied him bread.

Much more recently the ashes of the detective story writer, **Dorothy L. Sayers**, were buried under the tower.

Continue northwards up Wardour Street, among the offices of the film companies and businesses allied to them. **The Intrepid Fox** pub has nothing to do with the hunting field, rather it commemorates the politician Charles James Fox, called 'Champion of the People' in the famous Westminster election of 1784 for his implacable hostility to George III (p. 47). It is said any elector who voted for him got free beer here. It is now given over to dedicated followers of whatever is new in pop music. The Ship and the George are good examples of late-Victorian corner pubs. Sir

Terence Conran's huge **Mezzo** restaurant is at number 100, its two floors normally crammed with people 'circling each other like the mating eels of the Sargasso Sea', as Henry Porter put it. The kitchens are on full view, as are you and your companion. **Number 160**, formerly Novellos the music publishers, and now colonised by the British Library, has had its side aspects commented on already (p. 97). It is a classy bit of Edwardian Wrenaissance (1906) by Frank L. Pearson, with an elaborate cornice and five long, small-paned windows with varied pediments. Number 163, the Italian Graffiti Pizzeria, was where the furniture designer **Thomas Sheraton** lived. There is a pot of gold at the end of this walk, in the form of the 1899 shopfront of J. Blundell & Sons, Gold Refiners, Sweep Smelters, just before Oxford Street is reached at a point equidistant between Oxford Circus and Tottenham Court Road tubes.

From Oxford Circus tube, go south down Argyll Street, diverting into the **Argyll Pub** on the right for long enough to take in the numerous wood and etched glass partitions which have survived from the last century. These divide up the drinking area into a series of snugs and cosy corners. The **Palladium** theatre lower down was built by Frank Matcham in 1910 and has always been home to variety, and pantomime at Christmas. From 1932 it housed the regular Crazy Gang shows and after 1945 big American names like Judy Garland, Bing Crosby and Danny Kaye topped the bills. At its south-east end is a black Art Deco pile, once the home of the National Radiator Company, its decoration betraying the influence of the then recently discovered treasures of Tutankhamen.

The inescapable presence at this point is the Tudor Building of **Liberty & Co.** on the south side of Great Marlborough Street. Arthur Lasenby Liberty began work in the 1860s in something called the Oriental Warehouse, where Indian shawls and the first Japanese products that London had ever seen were on sale. In 1875 he set up his own shop on Regent Street. The first Liberty fabrics were a range of delicately dyed silks; these were soon followed by hand-printed fabrics using wooden blocks, often in paisley patterns. In the 1880s Liberty began selling ladies' high fashion, advised by the architect and aesthete, E. W. Godwin, for many years the lover of Ellen Terry. In 1894 it became a public company, having derived great impetus from the influence of the Arts and Crafts and the Aesthetic Movements on public taste. For anyone with pretensions to furnish their home or dress themselves in an artistic manner Liberty's was the place to come.

The Tudor Building is bogus down to its last beam, and the proportions are all wrong, but it is a wonderful relief from the

A crumbling frontage in Beak Street

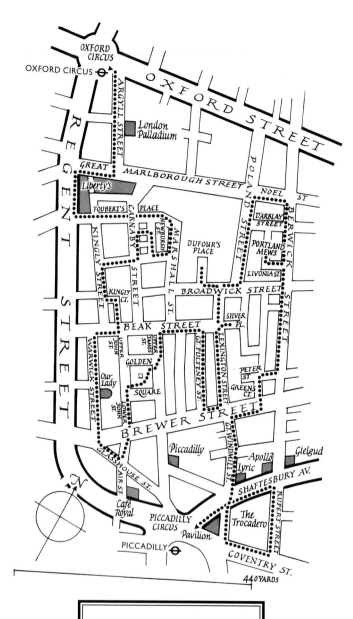

OXFORD
CIRCUS

OXFORD CIRCUS ⊖

OXFORD STREET

London
Palladium

GREAT
MARLBOROUGH STREET

POLAND STREET

NOEL ST

Liberty's

FOUBERT'S PLACE

CARNABY STREET

NEWBURGH ST

MARSHALL ST

DUFOUR'S PLACE

D'ARBLAY STREET

BERWICK STREET

KINGLY STREET

PORTLAND MEWS

LIVONIA ST.

KINGLY CT.

BROADWICK STREET

BEAK STREET

SILVER PL.

WARWICK STREET

JOHN ST

UPPER JAMES ST

UPPER JAMES ST

GOLDEN

GT. PULTENEY ST.

LEXINGTON STREET

PETER ST

GREEN'S CT.

Our
Lady

JOHN ST

SQUARE

BREWER STREET

GT. WINDMILL ST

Piccadilly

Apollo
Lyric

Gielgud

GLASSHOUSE ST.

SHAFTESBURY AV.

RUPERT STREET

Café
Royal

PICCADILLY
CIRCUS

Pavilion

The
Trocadero

N

PICCADILLY ⊖

COVENTRY ST.

440 YARDS

WALK FIVE

average Oxford Street or Regent Street department store. The
timbers came in large part from two old Royal Navy warships
broken up in 1921, the *Hindustan* and the *Impregnable*. The leaded
windows, balconies, gables, barge boards, barley-sugar twist brick
chimneys, carved surrounds to the display windows and golden
ship weathervane are all good fun. Above the entrance there are
four grotesque corbels and, inside the porch, linenfold panelling
and ceiling bosses. When in the central hall, where they sell the
scarves, look up at the open galleries, which for a moment make
one imagine this is the Globe Theatre; note the adzed rather than
sawn pillars, the plasterwork and ogee arched doorways; take a
ride in the lift, lined with more linenfold panelling. Outside once
more, look at the famous clock on the double bridge of sighs join-
ing the Tudor building to the block on Regent Street. The Four
Winds blow at its face; an owl on one side and a cock on the other
stand for night and day; on the hour St George fights the dragon
above; and above them again are two corbels in the form of seated
figures, heads in their hands.

Go out into **Regent Street** for a moment. You will have a slice
of Edwardian Baroque wedding cake either side of you, though
Dickins & Jones to the north is probably 1920s. Its ornament is
restricted to some snub-nosed lions with rings in their mouths and
stylised stone helmets with Egyptian wings, but Liberty's block to
the south – East India House, as it is called – has a mass of allegor-
ical free-standing statuary on top, above its concave, columned
front. At a guess it is Europe to the left, with the inevitable Britannia in the centre, and Asia (elephant and camel) to the right. The
best touches are the three figures above the rest, leaning over the
parapet. Above the street windows there are four seated bronze
Buddhas or oriental sages.

With the possible exception of the green-copper-domed
Mappin and Webb block, the rest of Regent Street is uninspiring,
so retreat back east down **Foubert's Place**, especially if you have
children in tow, because Hamley's toy shop is dangerously close.
Go instead to the London Kite and Juggling Company at number
10a which calls itself an alternative sports shop, but is really selling
grown-up toys. The lines stocked which are not encompassed by
its title include rollerblades, unicycles and sporting clothes. There

Liberty's contrasting Tudor and Classical skylines

is every chance that someone will be trying out the juggling stock. The Shakespeare's Head pub in the open area at the top of Carnaby Street is lively Arts and Crafts Jacobethan. The Subterranean Gents on Great Marlborough Street beyond it, where there is normally a gaggle of dispatch riders and their motor bikes, has an unexpected picture of the 1st Duke of Marlborough done in coloured tiles, on the way down. Beyond it again is the Magistrates' Court in good Edwardian Baroque. For many years St John Harmsworth was the magnanimous stipendiary magistrate there. One defendant called him a 'bald old bastard', to which he responded, 'Well, he's right on two counts'.

Continue along Foubert's Place. Numbers 29 to 31 has a terracotta first-floor bow window with an unflattering profile medallion of Queen Victoria, at the time of her Diamond Jubilee in 1897. Next come two good warehouse buildings in different shades of yellow brick, and a variety of stone, red-brick and terracotta trims. You are now in **Marshall Street**. The 'Leisure Centre' – in fact the old swimming bath – has a grandiose 1930s classical façade redeemed by the rather saucy supporters to the Westminster City coat-of-arms. Inside, the ticket kiosk is just like a West End theatre's and you can see the pool through the glass doors. Beyond is Blake House, a 1960s tower block with Cranks Health Foods at its foot, on the site of **William Blake**'s birthplace (1757). This poet and painter, the son of a hosier, crops up all over this part of London: for instance, going to a drawing school in the Strand, running a print shop at number 28 Poland Street with his brother, then setting up on his own at 27 Broadwick Street. He gave a telling example of his visionary outlook himself: " 'What,' it will be questioned, 'When the sun rises, do you not see a round disc of fire somewhat like a guinea?' Oh, no, no, I see an innumerable company of the Heavenly Host, crying, 'Holy, Holy, Holy, is the Lord God Almighty.' " When he got married, he and his wife used to sit in their summer house in Lambeth, stark naked, reading *Paradise Lost*. If friends called, Blake asked them in, saying, 'It's only Adam and Eve, you know.' In the 1820s, when he was still poor and neglected, Charles Lamb spotted his genius:

He paints in water colours, marvellous strange pictures, visions of his brain which he asserts that he has seen. They have great merit. He has *seen* the old Welsh bards on Snowdon – he has seen the Beautifullest, the Strongest, and the Ugliest Man, left alone from the Massacre of the Britons by the Romans. His poems have been sold hitherto only in manuscript . . . There is one to a Tiger, which I have heard recited . . . which is glorious . . . I must look on him as one of the most extraordinary persons of the age.

Contemporary Ceramics, which displays and sells the work of modern potters, is at number 7 Marshall Street. This area was one of the last bits of Soho Fields to be developed because thousands of plague victims had been buried here in 1665. Lord Craven, long-time protector of Charles I's sister Elizabeth, the Winter Queen, in his charity established a plague hospital in what was then an isolated spot.

Turn right into **Ganton Street** and out of it into **Newburgh Street**, all bollards and cobble stones and style-obsessed shops, but the houses are eighteenth-century, and as streets they are infinitely preferable to **Carnaby Street**, which comes next. John Stephen opened a scarf shop here in 1960 which began its transformation into the place to come for your 'gear', so that you could ape the Beatles or the Stones. Shops like 'I was Lord Kitchener's Valet' made play with Union Jacks and Imperial trappings to mix in with the beads, floral shirts, flared jeans and mini-skirts. It became the first stop on the trail for those in search of the elusive 'Swinging London'. Whatever excitement and flair it once had deserted it long ago, and it is now a depressing assemblage of tat, battening on the gullible teenage tourists, born long after its glory days, who still come, searching for a vestige of that brief period when British pop music transformed the world.

Take refuge in **Kingly Street**, which runs parallel with Carnaby Street, and then in **Kingly Court**, tucked in between the two. Cross Beak Street and go down **Warwick Street** to its Roman Catholic church, formerly known as the Royal Bavarian Chapel and on the site of the Portuguese and then the Bavarian Embassy Chapel. It owes its origins to the fact that these two countries had their embassy in the same building, successively, in Golden Square immediately behind the church. The embassy chapel was one of the few places where mass could be heard in the eighteenth century, but it was destroyed in the anti-Catholic Gordon Riots in

1780. The Catholic Relief Act of 1791 allowed the building of churches by native-born Catholics for the first time and those in this part of London decided to erect a church here where there had already been one, so as to avoid undue attention. Even though the Bavarian embassy had moved from Golden Square in 1788, the Elector of Bavaria went on subsidising the new church. It was much patronised by refugees from the French Revolution; George IV's wife, Mrs Fitzherbert, worshipped here; and visiting Italian opera singers sang, which earned it the name of the 'shilling opera'. Early in this century the Duke of Norfolk regularly came to mass from his house in St James's Square, but made a point of sitting by the members of the congregation from the Poland Street workhouse and not in the pews reserved for his family.

There were plans for J. F. Bentley, the architect of Westminster Cathedral, to reconstruct the whole church as a Roman basilica, lined with marble and mosaic, but only the apse was tackled. The Coronation of the Virgin there is based on his drawings, and the mosaic of the Three Kings on the side altar, where the silver votive hearts are, is also his. By the font there is a tablet in memory of Crown Prince Rupert of Bavaria 1869–1955, 'Head of the Royal Houses of Stuart, Wittelsbach, Tudor, Plantagenet and Cerdic', put up by the Royal Stuart Society.

At the south end of Warwick Street, the Leicester Arms is a good example of an ornate late-Victorian corner pub. Cross by it into **Glasshouse Street**, then pause for the view down **Air Street** through the rusticated arches supporting Sir Reginald Blomfield's slightly squeezed Palladian bridges (1923), across the Regent Street Quadrant, right through to Piccadilly. It was in Glasshouse Street that a bankrupt Parisian wine merchant on the run, known as Daniel Nicols, established the **Café Royal** in 1865. It soon expanded into Regent Street and by the 1890s its Domino Room was the place where London's poets, painters, writers and poseurs met to drink their absinthe and crème de menthe. The young Max Beerbohm was taken to it by the painter William Rothenstein:

There – in that exuberant vista of gilding and crimson velvet, set amidst all those opposing mirrors and upholding caryatids, with fumes of tobacco ever rising to the painted and pagan ceiling, and with the hum of

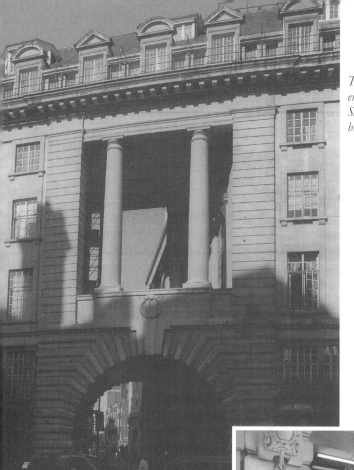

The Café Royal entrance by one of Air Street's Palladian bridges

An atlantes helping to support rival cuisines in Glasshouse Street, just off Piccadilly Circus

presumably cynical conversation broken into so sharply now and again by the clatter of dominoes shuffled on marble tables, I drew a deep breath and 'This indeed', said I to myself, 'is life'.

Perhaps it was one of the Café's waiters (as immortalised in a famous drawing by Aubrey Beardsley) to whom Oscar Wilde pointed out that, 'When I ask for a watercress sandwich, I do not mean a loaf with a field in the middle of it.'

When this end of Regent Street was rebuilt in the 1920s the arrangements within the Café all changed, with the Domino Room becoming the Grill Room, as it has remained. In the process its ceiling was lowered and the swagged, iron Corinthian columns were removed, but the mirrors and the caryatids with cartouches on their tummies suspended from garlands, which they hold above their heads, are still there.

Lower John Street has the premises of Bernard Quaritch the antiquarian booksellers, in an ugly white-brick 1880s warehouse. This leads into **Golden Square**, which began life in the seventeenth century as Gelding Close. On the left one or two of the original houses survive including numbers 23 and 24, which was the Portuguese and the Bavarian Embassy. On the north side, numbers 34 to 36 by Leonard Stokes (1914) is pointed to as a precursor of the Modern Movement in that it is not scared to own up to its frame construction (p. 71). Gables give a Dutch feel to the south side while the raised, paved garden with a low wall surround has an unfortunate suburban air to it and the pot-bellied, Roman kilted statue is the worse for wear. It is supposed to be George II and to have come from the sale at the Duke of Chandos' house, Cannons, near Edgware, in 1748, but the inventory for that exists and contains no mention of such a statue.

Go out into **Beak Street**, where Canaletto lodged at number 41 when he came to England during the 1740s in pursuit of his best customers, the English milordi who could no longer go to Venice because of the War of the Austrian Succession. It is easy to miss the small courtyard housing numbers 43 to 45 just here. This author was lucky enough to see Auberon Waugh, wine enthusiast and editor of the *Literary Review*, coming back to his offices at number 51 from a tasting with a half-empty bottle of Burgundy in

Running repairs by number 34, Lexington Street

One of the last of its kind, in Great Windmill Street

his hand. Further east there is a crumbling Victorian classical façade in the middle of a row of eighteenth-century houses, above 'Delicious Blue', an arrestingly decorated bar, and a few doors from John Wilkes, the old-established gunsmiths, who will mend your twelve-bore. Opposite them is a building covered in pistachio-green tiles (1905).

As you double back down **Great Pulteney Street** you pass the Sun and Thirteen Cantons pub. Apart from its name, it has an unexpected Gothic arched window at the top. There are some of the original eighteenth-century houses on this side. **Brewer Street** runs across the bottom and on the far side, next to the Victorian polychrome brick Glasshouse Stores pub, is 'Anything Left-handed', a shop selling just that. A passage here leads through to Smith's Court. In March 1765 **Mozart** and his older sister Nannerl were advertised as playing daily from 12.00 until 3.00 in Hickford's Great Room in Brewer Street. Leopold their father was at the door and as soon as someone had paid him the entrance fee, they sprang into action. For those not satisfied with a straightforward performance, they had a repertoire of special turns including playing with the keys covered, or sight-reading anything put in front of them.

There was an enigmatic figure living at number 38 Brewer Street in the second half of the eighteenth century, called the **Chevalier d'Eon**. Much speculation went on about the real sex of this former captain of dragoons, French diplomat cum secret service agent and fencer of renown. It was encouraged by the Chevalier, who enjoyed his notoriety. David Garrick wrote some lines on the phenomenon:

> Did not a Lady-Knight, late chevalier,
> A brave smart soldier in your eyes appear?
> Hey! Presto? Pass! His sword becomes a fan;
> A comely woman rising from a man!

But eventually he confessed to a furious French government that he was a woman. He was ordered home in that guise, but returned to London in 1785, still in skirts, and scraped a living giving exhibition fencing and chess matches. When d'Eon died in 1810, aged 81, a post-mortem finally settled it: he had been a man.

Double back northwards once more, up **Lexington Street**. Number 26 is the premises of M. Hand & Co., Gold Lacemen, one of those long-established craft firms that were once the bedrock of Soho. Without 'scrambled egg', uniforms round the world would be much duller. Number 34 has a good nineteenth-century wrought-iron screen above the door. It is followed by **Silver Place**, an alley off to the right with nothing special to single out but, as an entity, of great charm. Numbers 44 and 45 Lexington Street house Andrew Edmund's unusual business, which combines selling old prints with a restaurant.

Broadwick Street runs across the top of Lexington Street, and lives up to its original name, Broad Street, in that it is wider than most round here. Its two most notable features are number 33, an overblown post-modern block with high-tech touches, and a row of elegant early eighteenth-century houses, their doors surmounted by hoods on carved brackets. Charles Bridgeman, a key figure in English garden history in the earlier eighteenth century, lived in this terrace. According to Horace Walpole, it is to him that we owe that invaluable device, the ha-ha. He worked at Blenheim, Stowe and Claremont as well as in Kensington Gardens, where he created the Round Pond and the Serpentine. At the end of the terrace, look into **Dufours Place** where the architect Quinlan Terry has tried his hand at an office block in the eighteenth-century mode. (The lantern surmounted by a gold ball is highly characteristic of his work.) It does not come off, but is nonetheless valuable for so clearly demonstrating how important height is, in combination with all the other aspects of proportion and human scale that go towards Georgian architecture. The best place to see Terry's work in quantity is overlooking the river at Richmond.

In August 1854 there was a particularly virulent outbreak of cholera in this area. As far as Europe was concerned, this was a new disease, which had managed to escape from Asia thanks to the expansion of the Russian and British empires there. **Dr John Snow**, who lived in Frith Street, mapped where the deaths were occurring and saw that they centred on the public water pump in Broadwick Street. He persuaded the authorities to remove the handle of the pump on September 7, so it could no longer be used, and the mortality figures immediately dropped away. But it still took several decades for the germ theory to be accepted. The Broadwick Street well had become contaminated when water in which a baby's nappy had been washed was tipped into a cess pit three feet from it. Snow is commemorated in the nearby pub and by a replica handleless pump in the street.

Continue north up **Poland Street**. The Star and Garter pub on the left has no carpet, always a good sign, even if the decor has recently been antiqued by the brewery. In March 1811 **Percy Bysshe Shelley** came to live at number 15 with his Oxford friend, Thomas Jefferson Hogg. They had just been expelled from the University as the suspected authors of a pamphlet entitled 'the Necessity of Atheism'. Shelley was only 18, a 'brilliant young heretic' intent on reforming the world, fascinated by firearms, electricity and the state of pre-existence, even to the extent of seizing a baby from its mother's arms and questioning it on its experiences before it was born. When Hogg left him, Shelley had his first taste of living alone here: 'Solitude is most horrible . . . how inconsistent, in spite of all my boasted hatred of self, this moment thinking I could so far overcome Nature's law as to exist in complete seclusion.' He kept a journal of his dreams and this seems to have brought on fits of sleep-walking. His cousin Thomas Medwin recounts crossing Leicester Square at five one morning, and noticing a group of street children round the curled-up sleeping figure of Shelley.

The north wall of number 15 Poland Street, at the start of **Great Marlborough Street**, has a mural inspired by Shelley's 'Ode to the West Wind'. Its main features are a crouching Levantine youth and a split tree. Number 60 Great Marlborough Street, opposite, has a good weather vane on its cupola, while numbers 3 and 4, to the north, are handsome Edwardian Baroque with three winged putti at the first floor level. The middle stretches of this street are fairly barren, so go right instead along Noel Street before turning south once more, down **Berwick Street**.

This is the area for fashion jewellery and accessories; belts, buckles, buttons, trims, badges, sequins. Some windows are full of the sub-Wagnerian fantasy of the sword-and-sorcery designers. Many of the shops are, however, wholesale only, serving the needs of the rag trade nearby. There are eighteenth-century houses surviving here and there, but of no distinction. Turn right into the cul-de-sac of **Livonia Street** and then right again to see **Portland Mews** which runs up to **D 'Arblay Street**. Warehouses in the mews have been converted into offices and studios for the inevitable media firms. The Blue Posts pub on the corner with Broadwick Street has a distinctive corner turret, gable and green copper roof. Between it and Wardour Street is **Beard's Violin Shop**, in what looks like a former pub, with its glazed tilework.

Berwick Street Market begins at this point, with the King of Corsica pub amongst the barrows, named after Theodore von Neuhoff (p. 103). This is about the only traditional fruit-and-veg market left in Central London. The barrow wheels have owners' names carved on them to prevent theft. Turn right into Peter Street for a look at the former **Pulteney Board School** of 1880; like so many Board Schools, it is the most distinguished building in the area. Then left down Green's Court to emerge in **Brewer Street**. This neighbourhood is the only one where flesh is still paraded in any quantity, with various 'Live Shows' clustered round the Raymond Reviewbar. But there is also much healthy food on sale here as a counter-attraction: Lina Stores at number 18 is an old-fashioned continental grocers, Randall and Aubin are French butchers also selling charcuterie, and opposite them is Richards the fishmonger. Notice the framed certificates hanging in the butchers recording the war service of its French employees in 1914–18.

There are more barrows in Rupert Street, but instead go down **Great Windmill Street,** where the Soho Parish School, in Gothic yellow brick and stone trim, boasts a bust of the Earl of Derby. It is sandwiched between 'Live Shows', no doubt boasting more of the same. The old **Windmill Theatre** was famous for its non-stop variety bill which ran from 1932 to 1964. From 2.30 to 11 it mixed almost nude girls (motionless because of the demands of the Lord Chamberlain) with stand-up comedians, including Jimmy Edwards, Tony Hancock and Harry Secombe, who cut their teeth here. It is now called The Big Country, Western Saloon and Restaurant, and is part of Paul Raymond's empire. Next to it the leading obstetrician of the mid-Georgian era, William Hunter, lived with his dissecting room and museum in the same building.

Shaftesbury Avenue

*An Irish pub in a Victorian version of
Flemish Gothic, in Rupert Street*

The west side of the street has a number of good small frontages, culminating in the **St James Tavern**, where the carved wooden green men's faces at the top of the window frames should be sought out.

On the other side of Shaftesbury Avenue, on the corner, there is an amazing late-Victorian red sandstone building with balconies like theatre boxes, decorated with lions' masks and various grotesque faces. One particularly evil example is surrounded by bat's wings. All this can look surreal in the slanting evening sunlight. On the next corner, with **Coventry Street**, is the former Scott's Restaurant (1894) by Treadwell and Martin (p. 63). The overall effect is forlorn, but the detailing still repays closer study. In fact Coventry Street as a whole is fairly dire, full of tourist buses and fast food. In 1890 its problems were of a different nature, according to Rudyard Kipling: 'Through this shifting, shouting, brotheldom the pious British householder and his family bored their way back from the theatres, eyes-front and fixed, as though not seeing.'

A little along from Scott's is the entrance to the **Trocadero**, built from pallid artificial stone that looks like processed cheese, and converted into an entertainment and shopping complex some years ago, housing the Guinness World of Records among much else. It has never been a success and the latest plan is for it to house Segaworld, the 'first virtual reality theme park', and an Enid Blyton 'edu-tain-ment' centre. Nick Leslau, the man behind these schemes, recently bought her copyrights for £14.25 million. This will be quite in line with what Leicester Square had to offer 140 years ago. On the night of 8 March 1941 the Café de Paris, underground in Coventry Street, was packed with couples dancing to the band of 'Snakehips' Johnson. A bomb exploded, killing forty people outright. J. B. Priestley saw the rich dead laid out on the pavement, covered in sawdust 'like broken dolls'. Looters were soon at work, rifling handbags and taking the rings off the fingers of the dead and wounded.

When past the entrance to Planet Hollywood, home of the £8.00 hamburger, go back up **Rupert Street**, pausing only at the late Flemish Gothic of number 14, which has recently been turned into an Irish pub called Waxy O'Connor's. At the first junction turn left into Shaftesbury Avenue, where the opposite corner is occupied by the **Geilgud Theatre,** formerly the Globe. It is by W. G. R. Sprague and was built in 1906, the year after he built the Aldwych Theatre. Both theatres have circular galleries at first-floor level from which to look down into the foyer. What is regarded as the classic production of *The Importance of Being Earnest* was put on here in 1939, with John Geilgud, Edith Evans, Peggy Ashcroft and Gwen ffrangcon-Davies. **The Apollo Theatre** (1901) is enlivened on the outside by four winged, bare-breasted ladies below its two domes. Pevsner calls them angels, which seems unlikely. It was built by one Lewen Sharp for Henry Lowenfeld, who had the badge of a clan of German gypsies – a flying lizard supported by lions – incorporated on the right of the entrance, to bring him luck. Then there is the **Lyric Theatre**, built in 1888 by C. V. Phipps and so the oldest Shaftesbury Avenue theatre surviving. Lastly the **Pavilion**, on the left, actually facing Eros, does not really count among the theatres, because it was always a music hall, until turned into a cinema. Various coloured statues of Rock artists are placed on its façade to attract the crowds into the Rock Circus, an offshoot of Madam Tussaud's that it now houses.

Piccadilly Circus and the rest of its buildings will be covered in a subsequent volume, but you can use its tube station to go home.

A green man from the St James Tavern

INDEX

Italic numbers indicate illustrations